Praise for
THE WORLD IS OUR CLASSROOM

"A love of the natural world and an understanding of our place in it are vital for humanity and all other life. Knowing we are part of nature and not outside it is vital for the future. The importance of this comes across strongly in *The World Is Our Classroom*. Ross taught it by doing rather than telling. Experience rather than theory. This is a book that shows just what is possible, a book that gives hope for the future."

—CHRIS TOWNSEND, award-winning author
of *Out There: A Voice from The Wild*

"School teachers are largely bound by classroom walls and the Internet; parents have no such constraints. As Cindy Ross reveals in *The World Is Our Classroom*, the unbounded opportunities in nature should inspire every parent to create memories and powerful experiential learning opportunities. Significant emotional encounters can be transformative. When children are allowed to explore, and use their curiosity to discover the seemingly magical things in nature, it changes them as no passive learning can. In this rapidly changing world, we must foster a love of nature in every child as they must soon confront profound ecological disruption and play a vital role in restoring, replenishing and relocating elements of biodiversity to retain some aspect of system integrity upon which all life depends."

—LARRY SCHWEIGER, author of *Last Chance: Preserving Life on Earth*

"Navigating the best educational options for your children can feel like you are lost amid a dense wilderness. *The World Is Our Classroom* cuts a path through that wilderness and gives the reader a map of how to teach their children the resilience, compassion, and problem solving that is part of adventure-based learning."

—JENNIFER PHARR DAVIS, author and National
Geographic Adventurer of the Year

"Cindy Ross is one of today's most eloquent and thoughtful writers on the connection between humans and the natural world. *The World Is Our Classroom* shows how all of us invite humility and wonder into our lives, not only through great adventures, but through everyday communion with the rest of nature."

—RICHARD LOUV, author of *Vitamin N, The Nature Principle,* and *Last Child in the Woods: Saving Our Children from Nature-Deficit Disorder*

"We are encouraged to treat our children as if one tumble from the monkey bars or spiteful remark from a friend can cause a lifetime of pain. How exciting it is to see two parents put the world in front of their kids from such a young age, believing their kids will rise to the occasion. This book, *The World Is Our Classroom,* will explode some disabling myths about how fragile our kids are!"

—LENORE SKENAZY, founder of the book, blog, and movement Free-Range Kids

"In a culture increasingly alienated from nature and dependent on technology, Ms. Ross's book shows how our love for the world can be reanimated."

—AUDREY PETERMAN, president and co-founder of Earthwise Productions, Inc.

"Someone once said of Ginger Rogers: 'She does everything Fred Astaire does, but backwards and in high heels.' For me, that's what it's like watching Cindy Ross. She and I have both walked across countries, traveled all over the world, maintained freelance careers, and authored books. But in addition, Cindy and her husband, Todd, built their own log home with their own hands, and raised and schooled two children. Cindy's kids grew up with the world as their classroom. Want to live a big life? *The World Is Our Classroom* takes you on the journey of how one family did it, and it doesn't get any bigger, wilder, and better."

—KAREN BERGER, author of *Great Hiking Trails of the World* and the *New York Times*-bestselling *America's Great Hiking Trails*

"Cindy and her husband Todd have succeeded in accomplishing one of life's noblest goals—'to make one's avocation, one's vocation, as our two eyes see as one.' They have exhibited the courage, fortitude, and just plain old hard work, to create a life they fervently believe in and then effectively sharing it with their two children. The message in this book carries the truth born from actual experience. Read it, think about it, feel it, and then get on with making, rather than earning, a life for yourself and your loved ones."

—WARREN DOYLE, PhD, 36,000-miler and founder of the Appalachian Long Distance Hikers Association & the Appalachian Folk School

"Whether tightrope-walking a fogged-in Knife's Edge, ascending through the mist of Half Dome, or traversing slopes in grizzly country, Cindy and Todd present their children with breathtaking experiences that instill a sense of wonder, creativity, resilience, and self-confidence. The mental health benefits and lifelong lessons that come from extended time in nature resound through the book. Read this book before your children get sucked into the video-game vortex."

—LEO WALKER, president and co-founder of HIKE for Mental Health

"*The World Is Our Classroom* is an enthralling education in itself for anyone eager to intimately experience the mysteries of the natural world. Cindy Ross has given us a treasure of environmental consciousness, empathy, and gratitude for the life we share on this Earth."

—GAIL D. STOREY, author of *I Promise Not to Suffer: A Fool for Love Hikes the Pacific Crest Trail*, winner of the National Outdoor Book Award

"Cindy raised her family with a real consciousness of the value of being in nature and adventure. Cindy and her husband Todd have shown that getting kids outside early makes them better people in the long run and it makes us better parents. *The World Is Our Classroom* is not about completely flipping your life upside down but making the time to take you and your children outdoors. It's a lot easier to hand your child an iPad instead of going on a hike but it is ultimately much more fulfilling."

—COREY RICH, film director and adventure photographer, author of *My Favorite Places—Great Athletes in the Great Outdoors*

"*The World Is Our Classroom* is a fascinating discourse on creativity and learning. This book will help parents find ways to nurture creativity in their children—particularly by taking them into stimulating nature and giving them the freedom to explore and wonder. In these pages, parents will come to understand how necessary it is to spend lots of quality time with their children. Building a strong and effective hands-on relationship between parents and their children is the best way to minimize negative effects from challenges such as drug use."

—MICHAEL KESSLER, acclaimed contemporary artist

"Schooling, too often, is a world where teachers and schools are encouraged with 'drill and kill' methods. This development of a new culture of schooling in America seems to mean that 'successful' students must learn to operate their digital apparatuses and attach themselves to their computer screens, or else risk failure. The online computer-based testing begs the question about which priorities are most important; test taking on a computer screen or true learning from experience and adventure as advocated for by Cindy Ross's book, *The World Is Our Classroom?* Cindy's belief in experiential education for her children, in teaching children to have sense of place, belief in 'The Nature Principle,' and having great adventures is well worth contemplating."

—MONTY THORNBURG, PhD, educator and president of the John Muir Geotourism Center

THE WORLD IS OUR CLASSROOM

THE WORLD IS OUR CLASSROOM

HOW ONE FAMILY USED NATURE AND TRAVEL TO SHAPE AN EXTRAORDINARY EDUCATION

CINDY ROSS

ILLUSTRATIONS BY BRYCE ROSS GLADFELTER

SKYHORSE PUBLISHING

Skyhorse Publishing books may be purchased in bulk at special discounts for sales promotion, corporate gifts, fund-raising, or educational purposes. Special editions can also be created to specifications. For details, contact the Special Sales Department, Skyhorse Publishing, 307 West 36th Street, 11th Floor, New York, NY 10018 or info@skyhorsepublishing.com.

Skyhorse® and Skyhorse Publishing® are registered trademarks of Skyhorse Publishing, Inc.®, a Delaware corporation.

Visit our website at www.skyhorsepublishing.com.

10 9 8 7 6 5 4 3 2 1

Library of Congress Cataloging-in-Publication Data is available on file.

Cover design by Rain Saukas
Cover photo credit: iStockphoto

ISBN: 978-1-51072-956-8
Ebook ISBN: 978-1-51072-957-5

Printed in the United States of America

To my girls, Lee Reinert and Lynne Williams, who gave me the confidence and the tools to make the world our classroom.

CONTENTS

FOREWORD

A few years ago, on a travel writing assignment in South Africa, I had the great fortune to meet Cindy Ross. She and I were part of what we came to call "The Lucky Five," five women who, within twenty-four hours, were able to track and photograph the Big Five. It's every safari taker's goal, to see the African lion, African elephant, African leopard, Cape buffalo and rhino. Many go away empty-handed.

But even more fortuitous for me was the chance to spend a whole week with this remarkable woman. Cindy and I bonded almost immediately. We had children the same age. We looked at life in much the same way. We got up many mornings before the other three for a chance to walk and talk and share life dreams and philosophies.

Five minutes in, I knew I was in the presence of someone rare and unique, someone from whom I could learn important things.

So when Cindy asked me to write the foreword to this new book, I answered "yes, yes, yes" before she so much as put the question mark on the end of her sentence.

Because here's what I know. Cindy already practices what I've been writing about for the last four years. She knows the principles I shared in my international bestsellers, *E-Squared, E-Cubed,* and *Thank & Grow Rich.* Like I suggest in these books that have been translated into some forty languages, she lives in possibility state rather than problem state, which seems to be the dominant cultural paradigm. She knows about the butt-kicking power of the universal forces and she uses them to her advantage.

Cindy has much to teach all of us—about the natural world, about raising kids, about the truly important things that so many of us have forgotten as our noses get more tightly glued to our electronic devices.

She taught her kids, by unwavering example, that they should follow their joy no matter what. She taught them about science, spirituality, and nature, not from a boring textbook, nor from a computer screen, but from direct immersion in the very lessons they were learning. Their classroom for many years was the Continental Divide Trail where they witnessed spectacular displays of nature, their senses stimulated with double rainbows and night skies littered with stars. Other years, they explored foreign lands, exotic countries that most kids only experience in the pages of National Geographic.

From living with a Muslim family in Morocco to visiting the Swiss Alps where Heidi lived, their education was tasted, smelled, and felt in a way no child in a classroom could ever know.

While other kids in sterile labs across the country were dissecting worms, Bryce and Sierra, her children, were in the wilds of Kentucky peeling back the hide of an elk, cutting its ribs with tree loppers, accompanied by a wildlife biologist looking for the culprit (it was a meningeal worm) of its demise. They learned about nature by becoming part of its rhythm, by squatting on beaver dams and paddling through treetops swaying with gibbons on remote Thai lagoons.

But most of all, Cindy's kids learned that life's possibilities are endless and that absolutely anything can be achieved.

I am honored to write the foreword to this book and can say with complete conviction that anyone, from parents looking for child-rearing tips to inspiration seekers reaching for their dreams, will find what they're looking for in this volume of Cindy's unconventional, yet very wise words.

PAM GROUT

PREFACE

"And now," cried Max, "let the wild rumpus start!"
Maurice Sendak, *Where the Wild Things Are*

All along the creek were miles and miles of beaver dams in all stages of construction and deterioration. The children ran their fingertips over the tooth marks on pointed stubs of trees that the beavers have gnawed down and hauled away, some so recently that wood chips were scattered around. Behind dry, deserted dams, the silt was built up to dam level, making it clear that it was time for the beavers to move on. Further along the stream we came across an active dam and the difference was visually obvious. If we crouched down to eye level with the dam breast, even my one-year-old son, Bryce, could see how it raised the water level a few feet. The beavers built a dam right where the trail crossed, making our ford thigh deep; they were clearly in charge.

That night, our eagle-eyed daughter, Sierra, was the first to spot the beaver, silently gliding in the pond by our camp. She ran wildly back to our tent, so excited she could hardly speak.

I've spent enough time in the wilds to know that when a beaver chooses to emerge, it's a rare gift, so I grabbed the binoculars and cameras and trooped back to the pond.

Creeping toward the stick dam, we watched as the beaver chewed a willow branch in two with its sharp teeth. Then, sprig clenched in his mouth, it swam to the dam breast and disappeared. We waited; scanned the pond trying to guess where the beaver would resurface. The kids gasped when the slick, round head parted the water and the dark, beady eyes reappeared.

While we were watching the beaver, a small summer shower moistened the land, bringing a brilliant double rainbow that stretched right over the beaver pond. A golden eagle soared over our heads, its mighty head glowing from the setting sun. I looked at my husband, Todd, and we exchanged a look that clearly said, "These are the times of their lives. This is what we leave home to find." Sierra wasn't happy until she snuck barefoot through the mud to stand closer to the dam, where she watched the beaver swim back and forth for an hour. Not until darkness fell and her beaver friend retired for the night did she skip back to our campsite, saying, "Mama, today was one of the happiest days of my life."

Months later, we were visiting friends in southern New Jersey. We had just spent a few hours in the car and the kids were anxious to run around outdoors. Our friends lived on a quiet, rural road, and a large field behind their house led to an expansive scrub pine forest full of winding deer trails and hiding rabbits. A child could look at it as the gates to adventure, like C. S. Lewis's cupboard doors that lead to the land of Narnia—or not.

My friend, knowing our love for nature, was anxious to show my children their new computer application, "Acorn Pond." Her daughter skillfully clicked on areas around the pond and the animals came out and told us what they were doing.

When she clicked on "beaver," the computer simply said, "Beavers build dams on streams." I watched Sierra as a look of slight confusion covered her face. It brought her right back to our beaver friend—hearing the slap of his tail, seeing the light glisten on his wet fur, smelling the pond water, feeling the warmth of the lowering sun. The computer image did not have any of this.

This is when it hit me: how much we were teaching our children just by placing the world of nature in their path. Experiential learning is better than a book, better than a school building, better than a computer program. This kind of learning was creating a life for our children filled with abundance, passion, purpose and gratitude, and it would stay with them for the rest of their lives, because they had lived it.

INTRODUCTION

The Trail—Where the Learning Begins

"If things start happening, don't worry, don't stew. Just go right along and you'll start happening too."
Dr. Seuss, *Oh, The Places You'll Go!*

October 1989. From my elevated viewpoint on stage, I scanned the packed auditorium. I was looking for a child; no one in particular, but a small person. Just one. Instead, I saw bandanas tied around long hair, hiking boots on nearly every set of feet—people who clearly marched to their own drumbeat, but all adults. This was a conference of "professional" hikers—the Gathering of the Appalachian Long Distance Hikers Association (ALDHA), where workshops, slide shows, and information sessions showcased walking opportunities all over the globe. The five hundred people before me were hiking addicts who took every opportunity in their lives to walk long distance trails. They *lived* to hike.

My husband Todd and I were two of them. We had completed both the National Scenic 2,100-mile Appalachian Trail and the 2,600-mile Pacific Crest Trail. These folks were members of our tribe, but what I was looking for in the sea of faces was a child, for I was pregnant with my first baby. I saw none.

I was participating in a panel, discussing how we were able to create a lifestyle that enabled us to continue hiking long distances throughout our lives. When it was my turn to speak, I surprised myself and the entire audience by breaking down in tears. I asked for some wisdom and information from my mentors and elders on how to take a baby backpacking, how to continue this love that really defined who I was, how to find my way down the new path my husband and I were about to step out on.

I didn't just hike in my spare time as a recreational pastime. It began that way but I figured out how to turn backpacking into a livelihood. I wrote books about it, published hundreds of magazine articles, was employed as a backpacking teacher at a local college, was a guest speaker and a workshop leader. At thirty-four, I had begun to see clearly who I was and the work I was destined to do. Backpacking was my life and my job and I wanted to find a way to continue as a mother.

Not a single person from the audience raised a hand in response. I surmised that either my comrades made a conscious choice not to have children so that they could continue hiking, or they were older and had already raised their children before taking up this sport. After our panel, senior hikers tried to reassure me that children would be *such* a blessing that I would not mind giving up long-distance hiking. Most people believe that raising children is tantamount to settling down, living conventionally, and avoiding danger. That is not the vision Todd and I had of parenthood. Not only was the path ahead of us not well worn, it evidently did not exist. It felt as though Todd and I were attempting to penetrate a dense, inhabitable jungle. But if we had learned anything in our short lives, it was that we had to take the first steps to begin, even if they were baby steps, one at a time.

When our baby was born, Todd and I were happy to learn that Sierra enjoyed the natural world from the very first month of her life. It happened in the throes of a crying jag that just did not stop no matter how much jostling and rocking, soothing and singing we did. As a last resort, we took her outdoors, in the dark. To our surprise, Sierra was immediately transformed. She quieted, grew peaceful, and remained that way. From then on, no matter what the hour, the temperature, the weather, when she fussed, she went outside. It was not even necessary for her to see the wind blowing or the light dancing to divert her attention—a pitch-black night had the same effect. There was simply something magical about going outdoors that made her happy, and we used this technique throughout her babyhood.

Sierra was only four months old when we thought we'd give backpacking a try. Pennsylvania's sixty-mile Loyalsock Trail was her maiden trip. Even though Todd and I had each hiked over six thousand miles at this point, the endeavor felt daunting with a tiny baby in our care. We chose a trail that had road crossings every ten miles, as a built-in safety net if we found we could not do it. Although we had a friend's help to plant our car at the trails' terminus, our expectations of the whole family actually walking to it were low.

Despite our doubt, the Loyalsock Trail was a very successful hike and we learned how flexible babies can be on the trail, especially if their parents have experience. What we were amazed to discover was how naturally baby Sierra took to living outdoors and how much she seemed to enjoy it.

We watched her young senses open wide to all the beauty that surrounded her. She stared, mesmerized, at the sparkling sunlight on a lake. She listened to a singing brook and followed the wind as it raked through the trees and fluttered the leaves. She cawed to ravens and was so delighted when they answered her back. She discovered textures like pinecones, big oak leaves, and sand between her toes. When she woke up in our tent, she immediately rolled over and smiled before her eyes even opened. We knew she was happy out there.

When Sierra returned home, she seemed to suffer withdrawal and felt disoriented. She had to sit on a carpet instead of pine needles and noisy dry oak leaves, and had to watch a wind-up mobile instead of the wind and the dancing sunlight. She was physically separated from her mother and father when we sat her down to go about our business and do our chores. This was a huge difference from the trail, where for twenty-four hours a day, she was close to the rhythm, smell, and feel of her parents' bodies.

We tried our hand at long distance cycling when Sierra was eighteen months old—the 184-mile-long towpath trail along the Chesapeake & Ohio Historic Park in northern Maryland. The flat terrain, the frequent campsites every five miles, the excellent swimming in the paralleling Potomac River, the constant source of entertainment from the nearby active train line, made our introduction into this sport quite easy, despite the fact that I was five months pregnant. Sierra was strapped into a wide, open bike trailer with her favorite stuffed animals attached to cords and was able to observe the big world going by as well as get out and play and swim every five miles. Todd and I were feeling confident in our new lifestyle as outdoor adventuring parents, until our son Bryce arrived.

We were knocked back to reality when we attempted a mere day hike in New Hampshire's White Mountains. The goal was to climb up to the open Franconia ridgeline, walk across the alpine landscape, then circle back on another trail. But all day long we climbed steeply, as if we were ascending a never-ending rock ladder, with a child on each of our backs. Halfway through the day, we sat down defeated, me in near tears, knowing we had to turn around and abort our plans. How could we possibly backpack long distance with two babies when we couldn't even successfully accomplish a day hike? We didn't know it then but stock animals were the answer to our prayers.

Shortly after our failed White Mountain hike, our family was given the opportunity to embark on a life-changing adventure—llama packing the 500-mile Colorado Trail. The Rocky Mountain Llama Association wanted to promote packing with the sure-footed, gentle creatures and what better way to accomplish that than aiding a sweet little family on a long journey. Mellow, trustworthy llamas would carry our children on their backs in specially made saddles while spirited packers would carry our supplies, which included one hundred cloth diapers for baby Bryce. No one had done what we were attempting to do, and we weren't even sure how to do it. At first, our motives were purely selfish; hiking made Todd and me happy, and our one-year-old and three-year-old literally were coming along for the ride. We were not thinking of what the experience would do *for* our kids. But, as it turned out, this adventure would determine who our children would become more than anything else we, as parents, could have done.

In the first few days of llama packing, it became clear to us that this traveling life in the wilderness also made our children more joyful. They sat atop their trusty steeds and watched the exquisite Colorado Rockies go by. They walked when they felt like it and rode when they grew tired. They saw spectacular displays of nature from double rainbows to thundering herds of elk and night skies littered with stars. We covered about ten miles a day, which left plenty of time to climb on rocks, slosh in creeks, and skinny-dip in lakes. The Colorado Rockies became their personal playground. They learned, at a very young age, the thrill of adventure and fell deeply in love with the natural world.

One evening on the Colorado Trail, shortly after supper, one-year-old Bryce disappeared from our camp. I called and called, but got no answer. I began to check the area around our campsite. I found him a short distance away, certainly within earshot but totally oblivious to my calls. He was sitting in an open meadow in the lowering sunshine. A gentle breeze feathered the strands of his sun-bleached hair. He was lost in thought, staring at a purple aster in his hand as the wind fingered the petals, bending them down and then lifting them up. My throat tightened and my nostrils prickled as my eyes filled with tears. My goodness, my children must be happy out here, I thought. A sunlit meadow, a simple flower, an evening breeze are entertainment enough for my little boy. It quickly became obvious that the natural world possessed tremendous gifts for the child who gets to spend time in the outdoors. It stands to reason that when you increase the length of stay and the quality of the experience, the results will be even greater.

What seemed like an impossibility only a few short years ago at the ALDHA Gathering, was becoming a reality—we were evolving into a family that could successfully hikes long distances and Todd and I were joyously relieved. We were learning how to do it by taking those first scary steps. As an added bonus, our children were falling in love with our beloved sport too, all on their own.

On the trail, the fun and entertainment happened spontaneously, but something else was strangely and unexpectedly occurring at the same time—the children were changing. They were learning to be present and notice things, which proved, as time went by, to be huge.

As an artist, I had already trained my eye to be more observant, to notice shapes, patterns, light, and color nuances that an artist must be sensitive to in order to draw and paint. But I simplified this looking process down to a child's level and taught them to tune in and be aware of their senses.

In the early mornings or evenings, we sometimes got the children to whisper or stop their chatter altogether as we searched for deer in the open forests. We looked for squirrel nests in the trees when the leaves have fallen off. Along the water's edge, we looked for ducks swimming and turtles sunning on rocks in the water, for fish moving beneath the surface and birds in thickets and briars. We scanned alpine meadows for running marmots. In mountain lion country, we searched for trees that had strong horizontal limbs that were capable of supporting a large cat. In the mountain's scree slopes, we searched for squeaking pikas.

As we hiked, we looked for rocks with white quartz and sparkling mica or anything interesting at our feet. We looked for flowers or particular colors that we took turns choosing. All I had to do was spark their interest. On the trail, they learned to be present, to be aware of their world and when one views the world as the amazing, fascinating place that it truly is, there is no room for complacency or mediocrity. Once Sierra and Bryce began to really see, with their mind's eye, as opposed to merely looking, I knew that they would never be bored in life.

It did not take many weeks of this kind of immersion and interaction for Todd and I to realize that we were teaching our children. The learning was unintentional at first, although highly beneficial. It happened not just to their absorbent, young sponge brains but even for their parents, as we worked to engage them. It was also unavoidable. We couldn't help ourselves. We believed it was part of our job as parents—to show them the world and help them understand it.

It hit us one particular day in a large burn in the Sawatch Range. We took the opportunity to teach the kids about forest fires—how they start, what happens to the animals. We pointed out ditches that the firefighters had dug to try to stop the spread of flames. We looked at the rock-hard serotonin cones of the lodgepole pine, with seeds so tightly encased that they need the intense heat of fire in order to open. In the evening, we built a campfire and further explained fire to the children.

After that, Todd and I began to intentionally teach on the trail to help keep our children entertained and occupied. One day we talked about how trees grow, how they are able to stand upright, and how there are as many miles of roots underground holding them up as there are visible branches. We told the kids to imagine tiny straws sucking up water to the leaves. We encouraged them to use their imaginations and see images in their mind, a skill that often atrophies as we grow older. Of course, as a parent, you have to possess a sufficient amount of knowledge so you can share, so we carried field guides and learned together.

After our family successfully completed the 500-mile Colorado Trail in 1992, we were hooked. Why not have more of a good thing, we thought, and began planning to tackle the entire 3,100-mile National

Scenic Continental Divide Trail that stretches from Canada to Mexico through the Rocky Mountains, of which the Colorado Trail is a part.

We purchased our own llamas and all their packing gear, as well as a stock trailer. We returned to the Rocky Mountains every summer to traverse another 500-mile stretch. Mexico was our goal, and it took five summers to accomplish it. The Continental Divide Trail became Sierra and Bryce's first "school," during the most formative years of their lives.

No parent comes into this new lifestyle already knowing how to promote and nurture all aspects of our children's whole being. We learn alongside our children, through trial and error, for we parents are also a work in progress. There are a lot of surprises along the way and for our family on the trail, the laws of cause and effect seemed to be even louder and stronger. Maybe it was because the distractions of a modern, hectic life were absent. What was happening to our children was nothing short of amazing to Todd and I.

The first change we noticed was Sierra and Bryce's increase in creativity as they learned to use their imaginations. The summer that Bryce was three years old, I discovered the extent of his ability to focus on this newfound world of his. As he hiked, he made up rhyming poems about "Bonemen" and told extremely long stories about goblins and ghouls. He often walked ahead of me, spending as much time turning around and looking at me for a reaction as going forward. If he was telling me a story in camp, he followed me around while I did my chores. The most amazing behavior, however, was when he playacted in his head as he hiked.

A stick with a few broken branches would turn into a gun. For half an hour Bryce pretended he was a robber, shooting and making all kinds of mouth sounds. He found a horseshoe and held it with his shirt sleeve pulled over his hand pretending he was Captain Hook. For an hour he imagined he was a pirate, and in a deep voice made up poetry about pirates and recited it. He did all this while he was walking a normal pace of two and a half miles per hour, though rarely on the trail bed itself. Bryce's trail was frequently in a ditch, eroded by horses' hooves and hiking boots. He crossed back and forth from the trail-bed's ridge to the ditch, to the other ridge, and back down again. He stumbled over rocks and tufts of grass, putting in far more miles than was necessary, but he didn't mind; the stories went on.

Once, on the trail in camp, I was busy writing in my journal, when Bryce yelled from the bushes, "I've got bones!"

"That's nice," I replied, not even looking up. He made trip after trip lugging huge cow bones so big that he could hardly carry them. He sat down and got out his felt tipped markers and drew monsters on the flat areas (pelvic bones were best), planning on putting together a puppet show for us. He disappeared for more bones and yelled to me to help him. "I can't carry them," he hollered. "They are too big!" When he finally roused me, I discovered they were still stuck together, covered in dried meat and hair! He did not care.

Another time Bryce found a totally dried-up shrew and begged me to let him keep it. It looked as though it was frozen in mid-jump, and he felt sorry for it. I let him hold it by its hard tail just until we reached camp, if he promised to wash his hands. He named it "Thumpkin" and sang and talked to it, telling it how much he loved it for over an hour. I was amazed at what simple, seemingly insignificant things brought my children joy and entertainment on the trail, and how free their imaginations could run.

On the trail, Bryce was in another world. He was able to entertain himself happily and fully without the use of television, smart phones, video games or even man-made objects—just his mind left to run wild, his senses stimulated by nature, and his body moving through space. All those free hours, every day, to wander and wonder and absorb what he saw, smelled, heard, and felt; the impact was monumental. A childhood begun in this manner truly contributed to the gifted and talented artist he became as an adult.

Another skill I saw my children learning as we hiked was their attempt to think critically. One night Bryce and I lay in the tent, cuddling, and he asked, "Do you like to breathe in or out better, Mama?"

9

"I don't know," I told him. "I never thought about it. How about you?"

"Breathing in, because I can smell."

While Bryce indulged in the depths of his creative mind, Sierra discussed everything that was going on in her mind as she rode her llama. Sharing conversation was how she explored, examined, and made sense of her world. When she was only three, we played a guessing game of hers that stumped me. She quizzed, "What is Berrick (her llama) doing with his feet?" I replied, "Walking? Moving towards camp?" and a half dozen other actions Berrick could be doing, but nothing was the right answer. Finally, she said, "Making foot prints!" Of course! Moments like these showed me the kind of very analytical mind my daughter would develop, one that would serve her well in her future work as an anthropologist and a geographer, as she explored the world, helping to solve the planet's water crisis, and writing about it.

A school environment can teach children how to think critically but it doesn't give their minds the freedom to explore and it often falls short when it comes to opportunities that feed a child's soul. There simply are not enough free hours in a regimented school. Life on the trail, on the other hand, seemed to accelerate this kind of learning. On Lester Pass, in Wyoming's Wind River Range, we observed Sierra and Bryce's four- and six-year-old minds amazingly at work.

We crept around the edge of a gigantic snowfield that smothered the pass. Our descent appeared to be convex, over a dangerous cornice. We were forced to travel down the ridge about a quarter mile and find a safer route. The kids asked if they could hop off their llamas and lead them. The country was open, and there was no trail whatsoever. The way was cross-country and you had full reign over which direction you went.

We had to look ahead to see if the piece of meadow we were going to walk across would drop off and give way to a rocky cliff or safely lead us on to another strip of dry ground. We could possibly find ourselves at a dangerous precipice and have to backtrack and climb to another vantage point to evaluate a new direction. It was like a chess game where we were constantly planning two or three moves ahead. We had to hold about a half mile's topography in our heads as we hiked, for if our route dropped into a notch or a low point, we lost our expansive vision.

Todd and I followed the children closely and were amazed that their direction of travel was exactly the path we would have chosen. In all those summers of hiking, we never discussed how to select the safest, most direct terrain to travel across when negotiating a pass. Todd and I just led them, but they had been paying close attention, without even realizing it.

We saw the same behavior when it came to rock-hopping across a stream. Todd and I watched as the children selected stable rocks and judged the distance correctly. They planted their feet with skill and crossed with agility and grace. We did not know how much was seeping into their subconscious just by doing as they followed us all these miles. We did not sit down and actually teach them wilderness skills. I began to understand how profoundly our children were influenced by what they were experiencing on the trail without even being aware of it, how intently they had been paying attention.

Knowing how to negotiate a mountain pass and how to ford a stream are worthwhile skills, but would Sierra and Bryce need to know these to get through life? Doubtful. But more importantly, the experience was teaching them creative problem solving. By practicing this way of thinking, they would be better equipped to navigate a rapidly changing world.

Lenore Skenazy, author of *Free-Range Kids: Giving Our Children the Freedom We Had Without Going Nuts with Worry,* said, "Expecting kids to know how to make wise decisions and look after themselves when we limit their opportunities to do that makes about as much sense as expecting them to know how to drive safely without ever letting them practice."

Many of the things Sierra and Bryce learned while traveling on the Continental Divide Trail were acquired through modeling. Modeling is a way of teaching in which the teacher demonstrates a concept or approach to learning and students learn by observing the behavior and then imitating it. Teaching by modeling is often used as an intentional, instructional strategy but until this moment in our family's adventure, we were not aware that we were actually teaching using this method. But it made total sense and we were struck by the success of it.

Sierra and Bryce observed and followed us, their parent-guides, across snow fields, as we forded deep rivers, dodged lightning storms, hiked through driving rain, past wild animals, for thousands of miles. They witnessed our behavior as we confronted challenges, assessed risk, and demonstrated wise decision making. Their lives were in our hands and it was obvious to them, although they were very young. They believed their parents could and would keep them safe. They came to trust their parents, which would become increasingly more important as they grew older and learned to navigate life on their own. Most parents possess wisdom, and in order for our children to listen, believe, and embrace what we have learned, so they can make their own wise decisions, a deep trust must be present.

As Sierra and Bryce successfully learned these skills, they also came to trust themselves and their ability to make decisions. This lifestyle showed them how to work through struggles and have things end up being okay, that "this too shall pass," and the sun will come back out. Since Todd and I were fastidious about keeping them warm, dry, fed, safe, and loved, they were nearly always happy, despite inclement weather and other natural challenges. Even a youngster has a choice on whether he/she wants to be miserable or take the situation in stride and make the best of it. As a result, they came to not just trust themselves, but trust life and their fellow human beings, who were there to help us make that long 3,100-mile journey.

Trust is a very important thing to learn at a young age because it sets the tone for the rest of our lives. It can give a person the strength to go out on their own and live the life they were meant to live, to not see limits, and have a strong belief in themselves. A parent need not take their children across the Continental Divide in order to learn these things. Values and virtues can be learned right alongside knowledge and are even more important to an education than information and facts. But for our family, the trail became our personal path. For us, long-distance hiking was not a family vacation. It was an extension of our lives—our values—not a departure from life but an arrival.

Our family spent two months, 24/7, for five summers immersed in nature on the trail, and inseparable as a family. It was a most unusual steady diet of family together time, and our relationship grew stronger with every passing mile and every year spent on the trail. Since Todd and I were fortunate to witness and make note of our children's developments and learnings, we received insight and information into how we wanted to parent for the rest of their upbringing. We knew we could not continue hiking long trails, nor did we want to. But after completing the Continental Divide Trail, the bar for our family was raised unusually high. Traveling and the need for adventure and being immersed in the wild world had turned into a necessity, not a luxury. Because of what occurred out there, how deeply Sierra and Bryce were positively impacted, Todd and I were inspired to design a unique way of raising and educating them. The whole world came to be their classroom and we accessed it via nature, whenever possible. Our children learned through experiences and we taught by modeling, whether they were on the trail, at home, in the public school system, or traveling the world. What began as an actual physical path—the Colorado Trail and then the entire Continental Divide Trail—became a metaphorical path for our parenting and their whole childhood.

CHAPTER 1

Learning from Play

"Front yards are boring. Backyards tell stories."
James Stevenson, "Backyards," *Popcorn*

As I rummaged through the drawer of hats and gloves looking for matching pairs, I heard the teakettle whistle in the kitchen, reminding me to make hot chocolate for our thermos. We were dressing Sierra and Bryce in multiple layers of clothing. Todd and I wanted a fast getaway, for tonight we were going out to play under the full moon.

We first started going on full moon walks for ourselves, because we loved them and we needed these little doses of moonlight in order to stay happy and function in society. But after we became parents, we went for our children. We wanted Sierra and Bryce to see that there is much magic in the natural world and most of it is accessible to anyone. We also wanted to show them it was not necessary to travel far from our log home in order to have an adventure, learn, experience something new. Our long-distance hikes on the Continental Divide Trail set the bar high in our children's eyes. In between adventures, our base was our rural log home, the planning center. Every morning, when young Sierra woke up, she would ask, "What adventures are we having today?" I'd tell her of an outing—visit a museum, see a play, watch a documentary film, hear a concert, etc. If it was only a half-day excursion, she questioned, "What are we doing exciting for the *second* half of the day?" The answer was playing, or merely discovering the big world right where we lived.

Some parents might be nervous about relying on what is right outside the door to entertain, occupy and teach their children many of life's lessons. But given the right formula of free time, open space, a few materials, and a tiny bit of guidance, a whole universe of lesson plans is amazingly close by. Kids also learn to entertain themselves and not constantly rely on outside stimulation. Our family would go on many more adventures during the course of Sierra and Bryce's upbringing, both domestic and abroad, but for the most part, our home and their big backyard would be their primary source for learning. Much of it would be on their own, especially while they were young, and much of that learning would look, to the undiscerning eye, like play.

Fred Rogers (of *Mister Rogers' Neighborhood*, the hugely famous and influential educational preschool television show) once said, "Play is often talked about as if it were a relief from serious learning. But for children, play is serious learning. Play is really the work of childhood." Children learn while they play and they actually play to learn, without any help from adults. It is unsupervised play where they stand to gain the most. The American Academy of Pediatrics is of the opinion that play, especially outdoor play, is "essential to development as it contributes to the cognitive, physical, social, and emotional well-being of children and youth." Nearly every month, our family went into the night to "play" by the full moon.

We have walked under balmy summer moons in T-shirts, with katy-dids singing and lightning bugs flashing in a multi-sensory display. We have walked under autumn moons and watched migrating geese as they became silhouettes against the silvery disk. We have walked under spring moons and felt the warming breeze on our skin and smelled the rich earth waking up, and we have walked under winter moons, when the wind blew the ice-coated tree limbs that sparkled like jewels and tinkled like musical instruments.

Once we arrived at our location that evening, Sierra and I stood holding hands, thanking the sun out loud for its warmth and light all day long. We then turned and faced the opposite direction in the sky and waited to cheer the full moon in its rising. A thin sliver of the apricot moon poked above the hulking shape of the Blue Mountain Ridge. Everyone stood up and witnessed its rising. More of the moon materialized until it turned into a brilliant orange sphere. Todd explained to Sierra and Bryce that the moon makes no light of its own, but simply acts like a mirror, reflecting the sunlight back to us long after the sun has sunk below the horizon.

"Does the moon's face change?" Bryce asked. I told him that the moon rotates with the earth, but it does not spin on its axis like the earth does. The same side of the moon is always facing earth. We never see the other side, the far side of the moon. Sierra remarked that the moon looked larger and closer when it was rising. I explained that it is an optical illusion because it is so close to the horizon that the moon tricks our eyes into comparing it with nearby objects to create the impression of increased size. Through our binoculars, the kids got a close-up look at the craters and valleys and mountains on the moon, the dark patches that astronomers call plains and seas.

Much of the knowledge that Todd and I shared with the kids, we had gleaned from our past life experiences. If we did not possess the knowledge to explain and educate, we looked it up, either beforehand to enhance the experience, or afterwards, together, after we wondered and came up with a list of questions. The process of educating our children emerged naturally through our encounters with the world. It never felt forced nor boring; we were all curious and wanted to dig deeper and learn more about the topic.

When Bryce pulled out a red handkerchief on that moonlit walk, he was amazed that he could see color. Todd told him that without light, there is no color. It does not have to be sunlight or light bulbs; it can be from the light of the moon, which is technically reflected sunlight. These are the kinds of simple yet profound experiences that can ignite a spark in us, propel us down a certain path in life, without even realizing it, for it did to me when I was a child. It can be as humble a fact as learning about light.

I remember the first time I realized as a child that without light there was no color—the discovery that inspired me to want to become an artist. I was awake before dawn one morning, yet it was light enough to see the outline of the flowers on the curtains in my bedroom. I thought it unusual that the flowers looked grey, as I knew the fabric had orchid-hued flowers scattered all over it. Then, as if by magic, the faintest tint of color appeared. The color grew in intensity as the sun rose, until at last, the flowers were the color that I knew them to be. I was shocked to realize this direct connection between light and color.

As a parent, I made a conscious effort to teach Sierra and Bryce how to see and appreciate light and color in the natural world. These are the kinds of things Todd and I found just as important as teaching simple math and balancing a checkbook.

As we stared up at the constellations, a brilliant shooting star raced across the sky. We knew it was special to see a shooting star in full moonlight because the sky is so bright. Right afterwards, a great horned owl called in a nearby conifer forest. We cupped our hands and called back. All these events made the night feel magical.

Encouraging our children to view the natural world as magical was important to us as parents. Seeing through this lens evokes a feeling of awe, a sense of wonder. The wonder state often occurs when you don't quite understand what or why something is. It appears to be mysterious, until you learn the reason, the explanation, but the magical feeling often remains. It is a wonderful way to view the world and it ensures that you will always have the ability to be surprised and amazed.

I held Bryce's hand on the return hike. "Look at the moon shadows, Mama!" He lifted up his arms like a monster and yelled back to his sister, "I'm taking a moonbeam bath!" and ran down the moonlit trail playing monster. What fun we had on those moonlit walks. Some months we'd take drums that Todd made from deerskin that he tanned and stretched, and assist the full moon in its rising. We pretended we were Native Americans, filling the night air with our drum playing, until the orange orb surfaced on the horizon. Contrary to what much of the media and society would have us believe, families do not have to spend a ton of money on entertainment in order to have fun and learn. Opportunities to seek magical experiences and learning is right in your neighborhood. Sometimes all it takes is going outdoors and gazing up at the heavens.

Todd and I put considerable thought into the kind of neighborhood we wanted to raise our children in long before we even conceived. It was that important to us. Owning land was a number one priority. We built our log home on a low-lying ridge called Red Mountain. It sits in the shadow of the larger Blue Mountain, which is part of the Appalachian Mountain chain. The Blue Mountain seems to go on forever, as it rises in Maryland, crosses Pennsylvania on a west-east angle, then peters out in New Jersey. The Lenape tribe of the Delaware named this ridge Kittatinny, meaning "endless." Migratory birds follow the ridge and so do Appalachian Trail hikers, for the historic trail cuts a pathway along its ridgeline. The trail stands as the ultimate symbol of freedom for Todd and me, for we both fell in love with hiking and the natural world while traversing its 2,100-mile length.

In the central part of the ridge, the mountain makes a singular jog—1,500-foot Hawk Mountain sits atop this curve in the ridge. It is the focal point for the 2,500-acre mountaintop preserve known as Hawk Mountain Sanctuary, the first wildlife sanctuary in the world offering protection to birds of prey. Lenape chiefs were drawn to the point known as the North Lookout, an outcropping where they went to worship the Great Spirit. The Little Schuylkill, a designated Wild & Scenic River, runs through the valley at the base of the mountain. With the additional Pennsylvania State Game Lands and state forest lands, this area of the Commonwealth seemed like the perfect place to raise children, because it had an abundance of wild public land where we were free to recreate. The river and the mountain became Sierra and Bryce's playground.

To house and raise our children, Todd and I attended a ten-day log building school in northern Minnesota to learn to build our own log home from scratch. The class took us through every step of construction from felling trees, to chainsaw carving notches, to putting on the roof. We used a lot of salvage in its construction; my uncle had a demolition company, so our handcrafted home cost only $20,000. The bricks in our chimney were once street pavers; the slate roof was taken off a building scheduled for demotion that we hand scalloped, and most of our windows are recycled. We taught ourselves how to do every job—laying the block foundation, roofing, wiring, plumbing, building a chimney, and tiling the floors. Todd picked up the skills from books and helpful friends. With a background in fine furniture making, Todd hand-crafted all of our furniture, including our Victorian screen doors and the oak bed that I delivered Bryce in. Before we even became parents, Todd and I believed in lifelong learning.

Todd and I brought Sierra and Bryce into this beautiful log home built on twelve acres of open space. This unique haven would serve as the home base/planning center for our schooling. Inside, we are surrounded by art and crafts from paintings on the walls, sculpture on the shelves, stained glass in the windows, handmade braided wool rugs on the floors, a huge library of books, but not a single television. Even though all children are innately creative, our modern society has a way of suppressing this instinct. Many adults lose this ability and reserve the act of playing and creating (and much of the fun in life) for the elitist few actors, authors, and dancers. Picasso said, "All children are born artists. The challenge is to remain an artist as you grow up." Todd and I wanted to design a home that would encourage the creative act.

In the comfort of our home, we would research ideas, make contacts and network, and conduct the ground work for our adventures. Afterwards, we'd return home to record, build portfolios, and craft projects. Our library was massive. Supplies and materials for making things were unlimited.

The majority of Sierra and Bryce's "play dates" occurred on our homestead where they had a large organic garden, orchard, a surrounding forest, and pet cats, goats, and llamas to play with. They read books in the hammock and followed deer trails in the woods. When a summer shower occurred, they stripped down naked and danced in the rain. They slept out in their tree house, played in a large canvas tipi, and caught frogs with a net in our pond. On summer nights, they took showers out in the orchard in the solar shower, with the stars and the fireflies as their audience. In the winter, we fired up our Finnish log sauna and sweated with our friends. We built campfires and enjoyed every meal outdoors at our picnic table that the weather allowed.

Many of these things sound like childhood playing, but understand, something bigger was occurring in the underlying shadows. Sierra and Bryce were learning about biology, weather, astronomy, and natural history right alongside their play.

A parent has no idea what individual interest will grow into a lifelong satisfying occupation. Take, for example, our kids fascination with a place they created called "Bottletown." Sierra and Bryce found an old dump in the woods on our property from a long-gone, historic farmhouse. They played archeologist, excavating the antique bottles and pottery and using them to create the perimeter of an outdoor village in the woods—Bottletown. They each had their own space as well as other community areas. These were separated by unique borders of stones and bottles, strung-together flower-and-vine walls, and little pools of water they built. After they discovered an interesting rock or a different pattern in a leaf, the kids would change and redecorate, constantly searching for ways to improve and create more beauty. This play also taught them about boundaries, property lines, personal space and how to create it. Bottletown was like an ever-changing artistic portfolio where they could reinvent, be creative. If one of our children had an innate desire to be an architect, this imaginary town would have planted that seed. Regardless of what occupation they chose, Bottletown impacted their minds and stimulated their creativity, which would prove to be beneficial no matter who or what they grew to be as adults.

In our tiny backyard pond, which is merely a wide, lined puddle that collects water from our home's massive slate roof, our kids found salamanders. Watching and netting them, as well as North American toads, piqued their interest in amphibians. We purchased books on them and learned more. Todd found an old aquarium from his child-hood home and had fun creating a habitat with layered gravel, a slope to help them crawl up out of the pool of water and appropriate hiding places. The kids collected earthworms from the garden and learned to feed their new pets.

As children, Todd and I played outdoors as did most of the children raised in our generation. If we did not live in a wild place, we managed to find a corner, an edge, a space left open, to explore and discover. Our parents made us play outdoors. We were called home for dinner and then afterwards, went right back out to play a game of flashlight tag, remaining outdoors until bedtime.

The value of play is not always immediately obvious to today's parents. To some adults, play looks like a waste of time. In his book *Play: How it Shapes the Brain, Opens the Imagination, and Invigorates the Soul,* Stuart Brown informs that play is critical to brain development. This physician, psychiatrist, clinical researcher and the founder of the National Institute for Play has made a career of studying the effects of play on people and animals. He writes: "Play stimulates genes for nerve growth in the executive portion of the brain, the frontal cortex.

It fosters maturation of the very centers of the brain that allows kids to exert control over attention, to regulate emotions, to control their own behavior, all of which allows them to learn."

Through play, kids learn that they can solve problems for themselves. They gain confidence in their ability to negotiate life on their own. They develop coping skills and the ability to problem solve.

When Todd was young and growing up in a new suburb of West York, Pennsylvania, he and his friends visited the latest construction site with their wagon. From the trash pile, they loaded up with long, ungainly pieces of lumber, and pulled them for many blocks to the edge of the development, where their backyards ended and the woods began. There they built a fort. It taught them how to work together and think creatively as they designed their dwelling and discussed the most efficient way to build it; it taught them how to apply their math skills as they measured and sawed; and it taught them problem solving as they figured how to move lumber with fulcrums and levers. This all resulted from the play of young boys.

Today, there are far fewer kids playing outside. Drive nearly any-where in the country, and you will find that yards are vacant of children. The average American child spends more than seven hours in front of a screen and as few as thirty minutes playing outside. There are many culprits: the overuse of television, computers, and video games are much to blame. The more involved in passive entertainment a child becomes, the less he or she is able to focus, sustain attention and manage boredom and unstructured time.

Much of our philosophy using the natural world to raise and educate Sierra and Bryce sprung from our own personal experiences, but I was heartened to learn of author Richard Louv's groundbreaking book *Last Child in the Woods—Saving Our Children from Nature-Deficit Disorder* which reinforced what we already believed and practiced. The book focuses on the human-nature disconnect, highlighting the latest research findings. It connects the rapid increase in childhood depression and attention deficit disorders to this lack of communing with nature. As a result, a worldwide movement to get children and their families reconnected with the natural world was spurred. Louv began the Children and Nature Network (C&NN), a wellspring of information and knowledge (over five hundred studies) to inform and educate. To help alleviate the problem, a program of worldwide nature clubs for families was developed. If one is not located near you, the Families Nature Club Tool Kit was designed to guide parents into starting their own. Louv's book inspired Todd and I to continue on the path we had chosen using the natural world as a classroom as much as possible.

GARDENING AS A TEACHER

Long before I became a mother, I learned that a teacher friend of mine took her students on a field trip to the grocery store (although an actual a farm would have been better) so they could learn where food came from. On one excursion, a child admitted that she thought cows' milk was their pee. From that day onward, Todd and I vowed that our children would not only know where their food came from; they would have a hand in growing it.

Gardening holds immense opportunities for learning and food is essential for life no matter where a family lives or how they educate their children. Being knowledgeable about what you put into your mouth is fundamental information that Todd and I felt necessary to pass onto our kids. Sierra and Bryce should know what a genetically modified food is, why organic is healthier, what colony collapse disorder is, and how incredibly valuable bees are to our food. Knowledge is power and an uninformed consumer is a victim. Our garden was right outside our door and it was also a great stage for creative play.

In the orchard, Todd planted berry patches, a grape arbor, and twenty fruit trees. We grew most of our vegetables, and preserved our food by freezing and canning. We occasionally raised turkeys for meat and chickens for eggs. The kids helped Todd start seeds, and then misted the tiny plants with the spray water bottle. They helped push beans into the dirt trough with their index fingers and placed onion sets with the tiny, hairy roots down. When we harvested sweet corn and cut the kernels off the cob, the kids shoved the milky nuggets into plastic bags for freezing. We gathered apples and pressed cider and the kids helped by loading the hopper. They plucked golden potatoes out of the soil after their dad turned the mounds with his shovel and sifted them out with his pitchfork. Although it was truly gardening work, to the kids, it felt like playing.

When Sierra and Bryce wanted a snack, they did not search the fridge. Instead, they wandered out to the garden to devour sweet, red cherry tomatoes and sugar snap peas. They also knew which wild edibles they could eat and, armed with kitchen shears and colanders, harvested dandelion greens in the very early spring. Both kids loved wild chickweed and they picked it and added it to salads. Just to be playful one time, Bryce dumped salad dressing on a clump in the flower garden and got down on all fours and ate it like his pet goat.

The most important things Sierra and Bryce learned from helping in the garden was how to grow their own food. With this skill, they would never go hungry. They also witnessed the simple miracle of tiny seeds—how with a combination of rain, healthy soil, nutrients and tender loving care they can yield tremendous gifts. There are not many things in life so obvious. Here was one more opportunity to be awed by the natural world. Growing your own food fosters gratitude in a person, which is a virtue we would revisit year after year as the kids grow up.

To understand how important pollinators are, I took Sierra and Bryce to a master beekeeper's home, got them suited up in protective gear as they assisted in opening up a hive for observation. We visited a friend's dairy farm where they got to help out in the milking parlor, making it completely clear where milk comes from.

Sierra and Bryce also had a healthy understanding of where meat came from, knew that death was involved, but still wanted to learn how it was done. When Todd butchered our chickens, the kids stood high on a bucket to get away from the birds' flopping headless bodies.

They threw each chicken a kiss before their head came off and yelled to them that they loved them. The kids were curious, but also thought it important to be present for the creature's last minutes of life, a lesson learned from the Native Americans who gave thanks to the game they killed whose meat sustained them.

When Todd butchered a deer, they watched him strip off its hide and peel back its fur and learned how the hairs were hollow in the winter to trap in warmth. As we butchered, we taught them how organs worked: how a heart pumped blood, and how muscles and tendons were attached to the bones. When they were older, they wielded butcher knives and helped cut apart the flesh, seeing firsthand how the muscles were layered and held together. The process of home butchering gave Sierra and Bryce detailed anatomy lessons, because many body parts of large mammals are similar to humans. Later, when we processed the meat, the kids helped to make sausage. As the sausage stuffer machine pushed the ground meat and spices into the casings, the kids were surprised to learn that these tubular casings were obtained from the intestines of slaughtered pigs.

The present generation has become dependent on processed food and many families eat out at restaurants multiple times a week. Cooking from scratch is becoming a dying art. Yet, it is not only very educational to know how to cook, it is incredibly satisfying to harvest what you have grown in your garden and delight in eating fresh, healthy food. All our experiences centered around food production sparked an interest in cooking for Sierra and Bryce. After plucking our apples off the orchard trees, Todd taught the kids how to make home-made apple pies; we baked cobblers with our raspberries that the kids collected, pressed grape juice after harvesting our grapes, and on and on. They made up their own recipes and periodically orchestrated an entire ethnic meal, highlighting a particular country. It was one more way we as parents, could show them how to attain more pleasure in life, as well as good health.

If you want to build a network of like-minded, food-growing peers for your family, seek out the global network of 4H programs. These programs engage youth through hands-on learning to help kids build solid skills that help them succeed in life. Many focus on agriculture and livestock husbandry. A child can take science classes, learn to build compost, make ice cream, grow plants, raise bunnies, even drive tractors as a fifteen-year-old, the age a youth can legally drive tractors and work on farms. The urban community garden movement has exploded in the last decade, providing many opportunities for city residents to garden. In your own urban apartment, a balcony, rooftop space, or even pots by a sunny window can create a space for families to plant seeds and learn how to grow your own food.

MOVING INDOORS

Sierra and Bryce's favorite place to play and learn was outdoors but when they came inside, they played in a highly creative manner. I believe this was a direct effect of all the free time they spent exploring nature in the outdoors. They had tons of independent free time to pursue their own interests indoors, but I also felt it my job as their parent and education facilitator, to find opportunities for variety.

Both children were regularly enrolled in art and theater classes throughout their childhood. They were inspired to write their own plays and skits and choreographed dance recitals. Dinner guests at our home could count on an evening show with dessert. Sierra and Bryce also wrote songs after each outdoor trip that we took. After spending a week canoeing the Florida's Okefenokee Swamp and Suwannee River, they wrote and performed an entire soundtrack as a result of their experiences. I saw examples time and time again of how nature play directly fed, supported, and enhanced their creative indoor play. Many adults lose this ability and reserve the act of playing and creating (and much of the fun in life) for the elitist few actors, authors, and dancers.

Bryce developed an active imagination at a very young age. For example, when we walked in the woods, he would see "mice swimming in the forest." I never questioned these images nor challenged him. I was happy to see fantasy running freely through his imagination.

For my son, it was always art (and I mean that in the broad sense of the term as it included break dancing, spoken word/rap, in addition to drawing, sculpture, and book making). As soon as Bryce opened his eyes in the morning, he would make his way to the craft table and begin to draw in his pajamas. When he came home from an outing, before he even took off his coat, he would go straight to the table and begin to draw. No matter where we went, he drew. Before Bryce could write, he became consumed with making books. He spent hours poring over illustrations in children's books. Then he would gather wads of paper, have me staple the spine and begin to create storybooks. He would dictate the story line to me and I would print it out on a separate sheet of paper that he would copy into the book. Never mind that he could not yet read it. The books were often fifteen pages long with detailed plots, beginnings, climaxes, and conclusions that made complete sense structure-wise, accompanied with elaborate illustrations.

Besides drawing all the time, Bryce was learning to think creatively, and at the age of four, was able to articulate his thoughts and feelings. One day he came to me very concerned that his penis was "rotting off."

"Why would you think that?" I asked.

"Because it is all shriveled up and wrinkled."

So, I explained how it "grows." This evolved into a primitive chat on conception and birth. A whole set of new drawings resulted: a picture of a lady with warm glowing light bathing the area where a vagina is located, with arms of sunshine radiating from it. Just how you'll feel when you are a man, I thought. It was fascinating to watch his thoughts and ideas manifest into drawings.

As Bryce grew older and braver, he became fascinated with everything macabre—monsters and creepy things of all kinds. In his drawings, there was a lot of swordplay, eyeballs falling out, and animals devouring things.

He would spend an exorbitant amount of time on his Halloween costume each year, especially the make-up part, making sores and boils and sutures and gaping cuts with clay and paint. He found a foam wig head and inserted steak knife tips into it, pulled his jacket over his head to look headless, and tucked his severed head under his arm when he rang doorbells.

His friend's mother said to me, "Aren't you concerned?"

I laughed and said, "No. Bryce is the sweetest, most compassionate little boy on the planet. He cries when he sees a moth fluttering in the toilet bowl, and I have to rescue it amongst the urine and toilet paper and set it free. If he would ever begin to put these fantasies into reality, *then* I would become concerned. Since they are only in his imagination and on paper, I think we are okay for now."

But I did more than condone this passion, I fed it. I thought it my responsibility to supply Bryce's creative hunger, trusting that it would somehow help him do whatever important creative work he chose as an adult. I took him to every new animated film that came out on the big screen and rented anything from the past that I thought might expand his interest.

From the ages of four to six, Bryce draped multiple cotton bandanas over "scary" things back in his bedroom that we used for our home-school science class—an acrylic see-through skull showing bulging eyeballs and wrap-around facial muscles; a plastic torso with take-apart organs; a full skeleton dangling from a metal stand that had a blanket over it. He would remove their coverings in the daylight hours because he loved to look at them but covered them when night fell. He did not want to invite nightmares. But his favorite things to draw were the exact things little boy's nightmares are made of: the ghoulish, the creepy, and every type of monster imaginable.

His bookshelf was lined with illustrated books on dragons and wizards and strange sea creatures. His imagination was fed by writers and artists like Shel Silverstein, by books like Daniel Handler's Lemony Snicket series, by the work of Edward Gory, and later, graphic and horror novelist Clive Barker. Even in a "creepy" situation like a funeral, which most young children would avoid, Bryce found something fascinating. When Todd's grandfather died, he willing attended the funeral and whispered to me with wide eyes, "He's in a box, Mom, like Dracula."

While Bryce was busy drawing, Sierra was becoming very interested in textile art. She often played with my old Barbie dolls that I kept from my childhood along with a case full of clothing that I had sewn. When I was a child, my parents covered our kitchen chairs with red leatherette, and I took the leftover upholstery and sewed a fringed Native American costume for my doll. Sierra found this fascinating. When she was about six years old, she asked me to teach her to sew so she could make clothing for her Barbie dolls. She also made stuffed animals, incorporating beadwork and fabric paint. She got even more creative and began to design mobiles with Todd's help in balancing them. She found items in nature that she suspended with fishing line from a branch to make a large mobile for our bathroom. She went on to learn rug hooking with a friend's help and to do counted cross-stitch.

Sierra and Bryce's love of the creative process may be the result of all the free time they spent dreaming and imagining in the natural world. In the out of doors, children are not spectators; they are doing something. They are not merely observers or being passively entertained from a screen. Instead, they are engaging in what is known as participant observation: studying something by observing, taking notes, and, importantly, doing things with those around us. Todd and I were happy to learn from author Daniel Pink's book, *A Whole New Mind: Why Right-Brainers Will Rule the Future,* that creative acts and thoughts are increasingly believed to be what is needed most to create a better world. Pink has made a career out of studying and publishing provocative, bestselling books on the changing world of work. He found that highly creative individuals look at the world and everything in it differently, from a fresher, more artistic perspective. Creative individuals think in different ways and can help lead us into an unknown future. This became a very important goal for Todd and I as parents.

As Sierra and Bryce grew older, they each took their favorite way to play, in nature and with art, and began to pursue a deeper interest, finding opportunities beyond the home. Although both children participated in these activities, I could see how they were resonating differently with each child, propelling them down their individual path to do their life work.

When the kids discovered Sculpey clay, a type of model-making plastic compound that can be hardened by baking it in the oven, they took their "play" to a new level and turned their creations into a viable paying "job." Sierra created *millifiori* beads (Italian for thousand flowers), a technique originally developed from a European colored glass artform that's been adapted to polymer clays. She rolled, shaped and baked the beads, incorporated crystals and other beads, and made hundreds of necklaces, bracelets and earrings.

Bryce took the same polymer clay and made whimsical faces that he sculpted, then baked and glued magnets on the backs. He incorporated tiny pieces of boar bristles as whiskers and hair. He hand-painted his characteristically creepy yet entertaining style of elves on Christmas balls and made dozens of colored pencil drawings of caricatured people doing activities like climbing mountains or playing guitar that we matted and framed.

They were working towards a Home Show of their artwork. An artist friend helped them design and make their own individual business cards; Sierra's business was called Bead Girl, and Bryce's was Head Boy. Sierra stock-piled over 130 necklaces, 80 bracelets, and dozens of earrings. Bryce painted over 80 Christmas balls, 100 clay magnets and 70 framed drawings.

On the day of the event, the kids had to talk and explain to each guest how they made their art; they had to make change, wrap the purchases, record their earnings, be polite, and behave professionally. The Home Show was so successful that we took the remaining inventory to specialty boutiques and the Reading (Pennsylvania) Museum store and the shopkeepers carried their work for years. Sierra and Bryce checked periodically to replenish stock, do bookwork, collect checks and maintained a professional working relationship with the shop owners. Bryce went on to have his own One-Man Art Show at a local coffee shop, and the newspapers ran front page articles highlighting the thirteen-year-old artist. Over the years, both children made thousands of dollars of income from the sale of their work. This endeavor was not about making money, however; it was about learning to take charge of their life and their income, even as adolescents. All of this grew out of taking their "play" as youngsters to the next level.

BEYOND THE BACKYARD

While Bryce was clearly heading down the path of becoming an artist in his future life, Sierra gravitated more and more to the natural world. We heard of an opportunity at nearby Hawk Mountain Sanctuary to assist with a spring herptile count with a local naturalist. The children spread out across a patch of forest and walked slowly, crouching low, overturning rocks as they looked for salamanders. They discovered dozens of salamanders undetected by the untrained eye. They totaled their count and, with a special formula, were able to calculate the estimated population that this side of sanctuary's mountainside held. It gave them a hint of all the critters who are an integral part of the food chain and the web of life, many of which we had previously not even known existed.

There are so many things in our world that we don't know about, that a family can uncover and discover right in their backyard. Just drawing an outline of a small square in the yard or in a nearby park and getting down on all fours to discover what grows there and lives there can reveal an amazing world to a young person. Use a hand lens or a magnifying glass found in educational stores and online catalogues for even closer inspection. Borrow identification guides from the library to aid budding scientists in learning about creatures they observe.

Every state has reptile and amphibian monitoring organizations in place as well as many outdoor education centers that conduct vernal pool surveys and walks that families can participate in. They are wonderful resources for getting families out to discover nature, regardless of where you live or if you have your own open space.

After our family's participation in the amphibian count at Hawk Mountain Sanctuary, the staff naturalist was aware of our children's growing fascination with the creatures. He then told us of the salamander migration that occurs on a narrow stretch of road between our home and the mountain. In the early spring, the giant, six-inch-long spotted salamanders (*Ambystoma maculatum*) with the yellow polka dots move from their wintering grounds to breeding pools near the Little Schuylkill River. Conditions have to be absolutely perfect, as in forty-five to fifty-degree temperatures, light rain, and lengthening days. Armed with umbrellas, raincoats, and headlamps, we assisted the salamanders across the road so that they would not get flattened by cars. We learned that we should not touch them as the oils from our skin could harm them as well as their oils could make us sick, so we used a stick to guide them if a vehicle was approaching, or if we had to touch them, rub our hands with soil first. That night, we also ushered many large toads, leopard frogs, and spring peepers safely across. Folks who lived on that road stopped and asked what we were doing and although they had resided there for decades, had no idea of the magic that particular night held. These encounters were very good examples for our children of how to discover, appreciate, and learn from life right in the neighborhood. Our family's salamander study illustrates how we worked the experiential educational process: as parents, we first saw our kids playing in the pond; we don't know everything so we found opportunities to learn more and have our children interact with local educators. This became an ongoing, related, repetitive process, an approach to education.

When Sierra and Bryce were in middle school, their gifted program scheduled a saw-whet owl banding project. This universal scientific way to study birds involves attaching a small tag/radio transmitter to the leg or wing of a wild bird to enable individual identification. They can then monitor the movements of the bird and track its life history.

With a naturalist, the kids caught the very mysterious, palm-sized saw-whet owls in small mist nets that were stretched in the woods on the side of the Blue Mountain ridge. The owls were attracted to the area via a recording of the owl's mate. The kids carried the tiny owls indoors where they learned to weigh them and measure their wings and beaks. Sierra and Bryce were shown how to feel the owl's keel for muscle mass, and using a chart with various tints of saffron, they matched its eye color. Then they watched while the naturalist attached a tiny radio transmitter to track each owl's travels, before setting it free in the night.

Throughout Pennsylvania, eighty licensed banders and volunteers capture hundreds of these tiny owls, then harmlessly band and release them. The project is part of a continent-wide effort to learn more about where saw-whet owls migrate to. Nature centers that are situated near a migratory path operate a limited number of banding sites each autumn that folks can volunteer to participate in. Another great source for programs and classes is through your county extension office. Every county in every state has one. They offer a wide variety of classes and programs, including master naturalists.

Another favorite playground for our family, besides the mountain, was the Little Schuylkill River, which runs along the base of the Blue Mountain. Both contained a myriad of "lesson plans" for Sierra and Bryce and both were among their most influential teachers, constant educators throughout their entire childhoods. In the river, we enlisted the help of a fisherman friend to show the kids how to bait hooks, flip over rocks in the shallows to expose the caddis larvae underneath, and witness the hatch. Sierra fell so in love with fishing and the river that she and I took a class on fly fishing, and purchased her own tackle with her earned money. Bryce was happy just to slop in the river, building rock dams.

When we paddled stretches of the river, the kids learned how to read its surface, surmised what lay beneath and what influenced its flow.

They learned to navigate around boulders, rest in eddies, and power their own boat. They experienced the peace of floating in an inner tube while watching deer come out of the forest for a drink and an osprey dip down to snag a fish for its lunch.

Not every family is fortunate to live in a wild place near a river but there are opportunities to get your kids outdoors even in the city; for example, here in eastern Pennsylvania, our Schuylkill River travels all the way down to Philadelphia, where an urban family can also get out on the water to play. River towns often have liveries and outfitters that offer boat rentals. If there is a bike trail alongside the river, or a converted rail-trail, there may be an opportunity for cycling as well as paddling.

There were other desirable results Todd and I hoped to manifest from immersing our children in nature. We hoped the exposure would help to raise environmentally conscious kids who will protect Mother Earth, and ensure that the natural world will remain healthy and present for future generations. That cannot happen unless children forge an intimate, personal connection to the natural world. If a child has never played in the dirt to look for bugs and worms or encircled an old growth tree with their arms, how could he/she care that a species is disappearing or that our forests are being exploited and need protection? It's difficult to miss something you've never experienced. Children need to feel like going outside into nature is really coming home. Todd and I looked at the natural world, as well as our log home, as a sanctuary of peace. Here we found some of the best environments for playing, which ultimately led to some of the best learning.

NUTS AND BOLTS

You don't need to live in a rural area or own acreage in order to introduce and share memorable nature experiences with your children. Find a park, pack a picnic, and go spend a few hours outdoors. Exploring creeks is always a great way to introduce kids to nature. Pick a hot summer day, grab a pair of old sneakers, and turn them loose in the refreshing water. Utilizing local nature centers for family activities is an easy way to become introduced to nature study. Many have programs that are designed just for kids and families, offering free gear and guiding. There are also established family nature clubs in many states so your kids can play alongside peers and parents can get to know other like-minded families. Check out: www.childrenandnature.org/initiatives/families.

Parents can teach kids to skip rocks, identify wildflowers with a guidebook, build a campfire, and look for shooting stars in an open field during a meteorite shower. These things are free and will make a positive impact and lasting impression, much more than scrolling through social media on their phones.

A great way to start to get your kids to dig deeper into nature is to purchase a few nature study books that you can share and explore with your kids, books that introduce you to nature right in the back yard or in a small plot of green. Ranger Rick's *Nature Scope* books put out by the National Wildlife Federation and the *One Small Square* books by Donald Silver are good choices. Popular nature study books are excellent ways to learn and discover, even if all you have is the sky and the clouds and the passing birds. Remember that the best way to get a child outdoors is to go with them.

CHAPTER 2

Learning from History

"Each thing she learned became part of herself, to be used over and over in new adventures."

Kate Seredy, *Gypsy*

A CONESTOGA WAGON RIDE
ON THE OREGON TRAIL

"Hold the wagon, Jiggs, hold the wagon back," our driver commanded the mule that was pulling ahead of her teammate. My kids grabbed onto the side rails of the wagon as the wooden wheels rolled us down a rocky, rutted hill. We were traveling down the bone-rattling Rocky Ridge, near South Pass, Wyoming, the iron rims of the wagon wheels screeching against the rocks. Seven-year-old Sierra laughed and squeezed my hand, "Oh Mama, I feel like Laura Ingalls Wilder."

Todd read aloud every book in the *Little House on the Prairie* series to Sierra. The stories are about pioneering life on the prairie and the hardships they endured, through the eyes of a child, the writer Laura Ingalls Wilder. The heart-warming series have the power to make a child fall in love with reading, and perhaps history. The books provided Sierra with a unique glimpse into America's frontier past so she was especially excited for this next adventure: two days and nights traveling in a pioneer wagon on the National Historic Oregon Trail.

History was not my favorite subject in school, because I was never good at memorizing facts. Students were, and often still are, spoon fed lists that have to be committed to memory. An experience like wagon riding on the Oregon Trail was in stark contrast to learning *only* out of texts in a completely controlled school environment.

We got the idea for our Oregon Trail wagon ride when we were working on completing our 3,100-mile Continental Divide llama trek. Not only would it be a fun thing to do, it would make the westward movement and the pioneer experience personal to our children. Every time we loaded up our truck with gear and the stock trailer with llamas and headed west to hike a section, we felt akin to the pioneers. Todd and I often commented that these pioneers were really America's first long-distance walkers and we present-day, long-distance hikers, were also some of America's last pioneers. Since no other family had ever done what ours accomplished, and none since, we felt deep connections to these historic travelers. It only made sense for our children to learn more about the westward movement. And what better way than to have history come alive for them? Our hope was for Sierra and Bryce to come away from this experience with a much deeper appreciation for their ancestors.

We signed up with Historic Trails Expeditions based in Casper, Wyoming, which runs "prairie schooner" rides. Years ago, the pioneers used farm wagons with flat beds, and this present-day model was not much more luxurious. We covered twenty-five miles and along the way, helped take care of the animals, cook, and set up camp. It was an excellent way to bring living history into our children's lives and continue instilling a love of learning. Sharing these types of learning experiences with your children enables them to understand how far removed we have become from our beginnings and how far we have come since. Many Americans enjoy a privileged lifestyle and a good portion of that resulted from the sweat and sacrifice of our forefathers and foremothers. It is very important to know and understand how we acquired our good fortune and nothing quite informs a person like studying history—living history is the most fun way to learn. Reading books to our children, like the Little House series, is a good start, but we had to leave the confines of our home and actually participate to reach those deeper levels of understanding and appreciation. Our family's Oregon Trail wagon ride was the start of two decades of learning from history.

There are trails all across America that trace our people's movement, as they escaped persecution, sought independence, or satisfied their insatiable desire to explore new territory. They stretch for thousands of miles. Some are ghost trails, remnants of the past, paved over with black top for the most part, but sprinkled with history throughout their course. They celebrate and honor the American Indian, the migrating pioneers, the mail carriers, and the explorers. They are our National Historic Trails and there are nineteen designated by National Trails System Act in 1968. The land itself contributes to learning.

From 1841 to 1869, about five hundred thousand people followed this route of the Oregon Trail and similar ones across the Rocky Mountains to the untamed west. These folks were the restless ones, the determined ones, the ones looking for opportunities. Our route passed natural landmarks that guided these settlers' paths, such as Independence Rock and Devil's Gate. At one point, concrete markers alerted us to the fact that we were on the Pony Express as well as the Mormon, Pioneer, Oregon, and California National Scenic Trails! Back then, people were pushing west on these diverse paths, coming from different places, heading towards different destinations, following them for different reasons.

Some were carrying the mail, some fleeing religious persecution. Others were looking for gold, and wanting a better life and free land. All were forced to intersect in this section of Wyoming near South Pass. The reason the trails came together was to get travelers though the great barrier of the Rocky Mountains, and across the Great Basin of the Continental Divide. There were so many travelers in these parts that three hundred miles of ruts remained that have not been paved over, made by the thousands of wagon wheels that passed this way. This very historic spot in America has been protected by a 1978 Act of Congress. Their passage reshaped the west and displaced America's native people. Riding in a similar type of prairie schooner as the pioneers enabled even young children to connect to this powerful history.

Our guide told Sierra and Bryce stories of the land, pointing out rock cairns on the ridge line that modern sheep herders use to mark their routes. Each one looks slightly different and so herders have to carry binoculars to determine their exact location by their shape, and as a result know which direction to travel. They move the sheep eighty to one hundred miles in a season so these cairns are very important. Our driver alerts us to one lonely herder's shiny metal wagon on the far hillside. Most of the herders are Basque and come to America on visas to spend the season keeping sheep on the high plateaus of the west.

The history of this part-time population tending American sheep goes back to the California gold rush days of the 1850s. About ninety thousand arrived in 1949 from all over the world to hunt for gold, and they were called the "forty-niners." When these miners failed to find gold, they shifted their livelihood to rearing livestock. Their ancestors still immigrate to America and return home when the season ends. Some things about the landscape and the movement of people have not changed.

We stopped at Independence Rock and climbed 130 feet to the top of the round, granite dome for a view of the open land. The isolated rock formation was nicknamed "The Great Register of the Desert," bearing the carved names of over five thousand migrants, who were traveling from eastern America to points west. The rock was first a gathering place for native people and then a favorite resting spot and a beacon of hope to the pioneers.

We ran our fingers in the carved signatures, many in beautiful script. We read in the journals that many names were signed with buffalo grease and gunpowder. An early stonecutter entrepreneur set up shop and charged pioneers a small fee to cut their name in for a more enduring signature.

We thought of the families who buried babies along the way, those lost to frostbite, hunger, exhaustion, and other hardships of the road west. "Every seventy-five yards, from Missouri to Oregon, there was a grave," I told the kids. "One in ten died out here." As I gripped my children's small hands atop windswept Independence Rock, my eyes watered as we gazed out across the expansive prairie. I felt a connection to those emigrant families from the past. These sobering facts made me appreciate the fact that my family was experiencing this same trail in another era, but without the suffering.

In camp, the kids helped tend the mules. They unharnessed them, brushed and watered them, and fed them their supper of hay and oats. They looked for loose shoes and made sure there were no bruises from the rough stones of Rocky Ridge. We helped erect the lodge-poles of the Plains Indian tipi, our just-for-fun shelter for the night, and helped cook dinner in Dutch ovens over campfire coals.

Once dinner and chores were completed, our hosts taught Sierra and Bryce how to make bows and arrows out of aspen twigs and twine and accurately shoot them. We climbed a nearby hill for the sunset and Bryce pointed. "Look Mom, wild horses," which were galloping freely less than a mile away. I told the kids that horses were brought here by the Europeans, that they were not indigenous, but were incorporated into the Native Americans' way of life and some, like these, became wild.

I told the kids that in some spots on the Oregon Trail, the wagons might have been twenty across as drivers spread out to avoid eating one another's dust. One of the journals we carried, written by a pioneer woman, read, "Dust is two to three inches in depth and as fine as flour. We cannot see the wagons next to us and at times cannot even see the mules." We tried to imagine the scene from our perch on the rock above our camp, smell the dust instead of the sage-filled evening air. In our tent at night, we read aloud to one another. I supplemented Sierra and Bryce's experiential education with books on the westward movement to ground them in literature and history. One informed and complemented the other.

We concluded our two-day wagon ride in South Pass by overnighting in the 120-year-old Miner's Cabin Inn, its windows illuminated by candles. Our bedroom had a pitcher and bowl for washing, like in the forty-niners' day, with a community bathroom down the hall. Over dinner, our host played her grandmother's very old LP records on the turntable to the kids' delight: "Tumbleweed" and "Home on the Range," by the Singing Cowboy, Gene Autry.

After breakfast the next morning, armed with colanders and pans, our host's geologist son took Sierra and Bryce to the creek out back where he had dug a hole. "Gold nuggets are very heavy and they work their way down," he informed them. He taught them how to swirl the mix of water and fine gravel. He explained that for a handful of years, the gold rush and the westward expansion were happening simultaneously. Some traveled west in hopes of finding gold, but resorted to farming Oregon's land when they didn't hit the mother lode.

The Oregon Trail is just one National Historic Trail, and our three-day wagon ride was a tiny taste of what is available for the adventurer and history lover. One would need multiple lifetimes to explore them all.

Our family's love of history began in Sierra's little twin bed, with her father crowding in, both heads sharing the same pillow, as they read aloud from the Little House on the Prairie books. Reading first initiated an interest in history but all the experiences that came afterwards were *intentional*; our inspiration was followed by exploration. This was the same way our eyes were first opened to learning on the Continental Divide Trail, by accident. Todd and I went on to design an education for our children that valued and embedded these living history experiences into daily life, whether it was while home schooling or alongside public education. After the Oregon Trail, we all wanted more experiences where we could be actual participants in living history events. We did not have to travel far from home to find them.

PENNSYLVANIA GOSHENHOPPEN

For over fifty years, one of the most authentic Pennsylvania German folk festivals in America is held in Pennsylvania, in the southeastern part of the state, where one of the oldest continuously existing Pennsylvania German communities still thrives. During the Goshenhoppen festival, more than one thousand costumed volunteers share the secrets of their vanishing trades and arts as well as prepare food much like their Pennsylvania German ancestors would have done.

Todd's patriarchal side of his family has accurately traced their ancestors back to the German/Swiss border to the town of Glatfetten on the river Glat. They came to America back in the 1600s and found the fertile lands of Pennsylvania very similar to their home in Europe and perfect for their life of farming. Learning about the history and culture of Todd's people was very important to our family and the Goshenhoppen Festival helped. After we attended, we were hungry for more and were excited to learn that Sierra and Bryce could sign up and be student apprentices, and so we returned.

When the kids checked in, they were given a traditional costume to wear, then went to their assigned jobs: Sierra to help make German meals that were commonly served in the 1800s; Bryce to help deliver hay and block ice. This is what children back in this era would have helped with.

At the festival, women roasted whole chickens on a cord over an open fire, strung green beans to dry, made molasses cookies, and slid loaves of bread out of ovens. There was schnitz (dried apple) pie to sample, potato-filled pig's stomach, spiced mead made with honey, and fried corn meal mush. One stand offered potato candy and explained that on Sundays, children would combine leftover mashed potatoes with butter, vanilla, and confectioner's sugar and roll them into balls to make a treat that tastes like cake icing.

"In some families, cooking was the only activity allowed on the Sabbath, besides feeding animals," one of the costumed girls told us. "They could read the Bible, but children couldn't play unless it was with Noah's Ark animals or making potato candy."

Besides the outdoor kitchens, there were seamstresses, spinners, cigar makers, dowsers, broom makers, stone masons, furniture craftsmen, paper makers, and basket weavers. Visitors watched chair making, quill pen demonstrations, gunsmithing, rug braiding, fence post boring, blacksmithing, thatching, and tinsmithing. Visitors observed the Pennsylvania German food, scrapple, being processed from start to finish, beginning with the butchering of a pig. Another thing Sierra and Bryce observed was the division of labor between the sexes. The gender role/division of labor was not something our kids put much thought into growing up. They knew their mother helped to build their log home right alongside Dad, used her own chainsaw, and did the heavy work too. And that Dad also changed their cloth diapers, and put in his share of time in the kitchen as he is the pie and bread baker in the family. Our family had a discussion about how clear-cut role division back in the 1800s worked for them but how it appears quite limiting today.

Sounds of the village surrounded us, making us feel as though we had stepped back in time. Young girls herded flocks of geese, bands played German music, wagons delivered milk cans of water, and ragmen visited women to purchase discarded fabric and clothing. A woman rode by sitting sidesaddle on a horse, and young boys, like Bryce, used metal tongs to deliver ice blocks. Here was essentially a village, a society reconstructed, that one could walk through and learn from. It was different than actually traveling *through* a historical landscape like on our Oregon Trail wagon ride where we read the signs of history.

Sierra wrote of her experience:

Our kitchen and dining room which were open-aired, had panel-like walls with doors just like the inside of a house but with no roof. We had cupboards and dishes, a dining room table, an ornate cast iron wood cook stove, a porch with rocking chairs, and even rugs rolled out in the grass. It felt like we were in a life-size dollhouse!

The first meal of the day was breakfast, consisting of fried potatoes, summer sausage and gravy, AP cake, rye bread with homemade apple butter, and cottage cheese pie. For dinner, we made corn fried in lard with eggs, a giant potato stuffed noodle called Boova Shenkel that was boiled and fried, a ground cheery (cherry) pie made with a strange, sweet, yellow fruit that resembled a tomato which we had husked earlier from its paper-thin shell. Our leader blew a conch shell to trumpet the call to eat and we served a table full of exhibitors and visitors and scooped up the leftovers in tiny cups to feed passing visitors.

In between meals, there was plenty of time to walk around and see the rest of the festival and the demonstrations. It was an exhausting day. After eight hours cooking at wood stoves wearing a double layer, ankle length, long sleeved dress in scorching summer heat, I was beat, but it really gave me an appreciation for the hard work that women in the past went through just to get a meal on the table!

Here in the Mid-Atlantic, we are fortunate to have many historic sites and events honoring and showcasing the past. Pennsylvania, like most states, has a Historical and Museum Commission (PHMC), which is the official history agency of the Commonwealth. On their site, they list all the state museums and trails of history. You can surf the site and discover events where living history is portrayed. Many offer classes that the public is invited to participate in, and have special programs just for children. At Daniel Boone Homestead in Pennsylvania, for example, you can learn to weave on a loom that once belonged to Daniel Boone's mother, bake in an outdoor oven, dip candles, and learn to identify and gather wild edibles and combine them into a meal that is cooked over a fire.

Scout troops and church youth groups might also include field trips to historic sites. I learned that the Battleship New Jersey, docked in the Delaware River, offers encampments for groups, where they experience taps in the morning, eat in the ship's mess hall, and get a ride in a 4-D simulator, which features exciting 3-D visuals and air blasts. Our local scout troop toured the Naval Academy in Annapolis, Maryland, where they learned about its history and attended a football game. The troop leader also took the scouts up the cog railroad on Mount Washington in New Hampshire, to learn about weather patterns, the history of the station, and the cog railroad.

LONG RIFLE RENDEZVOUS

When we learned that Todd's Aunt Brenda and Uncle Donny participate in an annual Long Rifle Rendezvous, we wanted to be a part of this living history event for our children's education. Between 1740 to 1840, the American Mountain Man roamed North America's forests harvesting beaver pelts. These rough wilderness men gathered together on an annual basis to trade, sell, and barter for items like guns, skins, and jewelry, in exchange for their pelts. Rendezvous were held across the northern tier of America and lasted anywhere from several days to a few months. Modern-day events commemorating these historic gatherings are now held to recreate the culture, technology, and livelihood of this era and preserve the historical legacy.

During the festival, all clothing, accoutrements, and camp gear must reflect this historic period. Todd's relatives own a white canvas wall tent, period outfits, and the campfire cooking utensils his uncle made in the blacksmith forge. Nothing modern is allowed, not even sunglasses or zippers. There are no aluminum tent poles, no Coleman stoves or coolers, no Teflon pans or plastic. Sierra wore a long cotton skirt and a bonnet; Bryce wore britches and a linen shirt and vest.

Wood smoke from the many cook fires hung in the air, thick and pungent. In the distance, the rapid gunfire from a flintlock shattered the peace and competed with the mournful sound of bagpipes. Women hand sewed, spun, wove, knitted, and made cording. Children painted wooden beads and wooden figures, participated in period games like tug of war and tomahawk toss, and listened to Native American stories. Men set up traps and snares, and made fires by friction using a bow drill. Not a smartphone was in sight.

Throughout the day, there were music workshops to attend and the popular Highland Games to participate in, like tossing sheaves of grain or tall wooden timbers called capers. You could shop for knives with handles made from a raccoon's jaw with the teeth still in them, toothbrushes made from licorice roots, slingshots, leatherwear, and hard cakes of tea like those thrown overboard during the Boston Tea Party. Just walking through the encampment, which is open to the public, allows you to get a taste of life as it once was. An event like this creates a space that one can occupy and explore questions within and about history.

On the last night of the rendezvous weekend, we roasted venison over a fire, baked bread in a Dutch oven, and walked through camp with a candle lantern, chatting with the frontier folk. We fell asleep to firelight flickering on the white canvas, listening to the sweet dulcimer and fiddle music in the distance. Although our ancestors may not have had choices in the way they lived, we can decide to bring back a skill or an activity to improve the quality of our present lives, such as the joy of working with your hands, cooking from scratch, feeling the peace of a campfire, and making live music. These living history experiences remind us of what might have been lost and what we have the ability to bring back to enrich our lives, once we are made aware of them.

Reenactments and living history are, in a sense, playacting and are certainly not real, but they do provide a portal that enables us to get inside a time period and experience it. The same goes with reading historical fiction. It is not fact, yet reading it can provide an entry point into real research and study. Wilder's books were based on her life and, even though they were technically fiction, she made the characters and their life and times accessible. In the life of a young impressive child, the ability to relate can have a great impact.

AN OJIBWA INDIAN VILLAGE/FUR TRADING POSTS

Our family always had our radar on for unique educational experiences. While traveling to Wisconsin on a river trip one year, we stopped for a short visit at the Forts Folle Avoine Historical Park in Danbury, Wisconsin. This National Historic site is significant and unique because it is the only place on the North American continent where two competing fur trading companies were in very close proximity to one another. More than a hundred small trading posts like this one were sprinkled across the North Woods and into Canada. Native Americans harvested furs in the winter and brought them here on horseback and raft to trade with Europeans for items like copper kettles and metal tools. The fur pelts were shipped to the big depots in colossal birch-bark canoes manned by voyageurs. There they were counted, pressed, and sent east to be made into sought-after beaver felt hats and fur coats. Unlike the Long Rifle Rendezvous and other staged encampments that illustrated a period in history, and are temporary, this recreated village is all about a sense of place, for what is illustrated in Forts Folle Avoine is very close to what actually occurred here many years ago.

After a few years of servicing the trappers and the traders here at Forts Folle, things ended badly, with the post and village burning to the ground. Wood rots but buried burned wood survives. After two hundred years, archeologists were able to find this pure, untouched site and on the original footprint, rebuilt the posts that once existed.

We were so impressed with the fascinating story of the Ojibwa Indian village and forts that we asked the park managers if we could return and participate in a service project. They welcomed us the following year. The kids and I were given a rare glimpse into Ojibwa life as it was back in the days of the fur traders' rendezvous.

I lay on my back in the firelight and listened to the pinging rain on the roof overhead. It sounded different from rain on a tin roof or nylon tent wall, for these raindrops bounced off dried birch bark. Sierra and Bryce were stretched around the perimeter of the Ojibwa council lodge, reading and writing in their journals. Beeswax candles in lanterns added light to the warm glow of the crackling fire. Beneath us were rabbit pelts and beaver skins, warding off the earth's dampness. The musky scent of the animal hides mixed with the wood smoke. From where we lay in the lodge, I could see the cooking arbor and the drying and smoking racks. There were eight different structures outside the door. Behind the village was a log palisade surrounding three log cabins—the fur-trading store and lodging for the company's merchants.

For dinner, we purchased wild rice, dried cranberries, and maple syrup crystals from the gift shop to add to our Northwood's stew: squash, mushrooms, nuts, and apples. Using rolls of birch bark as kneeling pads, stirring with the hipbone of a deer, we prepared our stew in a cast-iron kettle over the open fire. To clean it, we took the iron pot to a clearing of white sand and scrubbed it with horsetail sprigs, like the Native Americans did.

The kids slid small sticks under the pot, keeping the fire going, and tended the fire in our lodge. They wrapped kindling sticks in birch bark for quick flare-ups and to restart our morning fire. We passed the evening the way indigenous peoples would have done two hundred years ago: playing cards and dice games by firelight. Come dawn, morning light and a patch of blue sky shone through the smoke hole of the wigwam, alerting us to start our day.

The next day's service project entailed sloughing off the rust-colored pine-bough roof used to shade the village's precious birch-bark canoe. Sierra and Bryce ascended ladders, climbed around the framework, and layered fresh, sweet-smelling green boughs to make a new roof. They shared, "Just replacing the pine bough roof gave us an appreciation of how much work went into making a Native American village, especially since years ago, they moved it four times a year." Through our participation, we reached a deeper layer of understanding of how the Ojibwa lived and what went into maintaining their lifestyle.

We also had the satisfaction of actually giving something back to this community, making us feel less like takers and more like contributors, especially in light of how much was historically stolen from America's native people. It made our presence at the park feel more valid. Todd and I felt that the practice of giving back in some way should be an essential part of our children's education and we looked to create opportunities wherever possible. This satisfies the goal of what learning from living history ultimately is—a portal to a greater appreciation and a deeper gratitude for who and what came before us.

A local Ojibwa Indian named Magwa, who was employed by the historic park, showed the kids how to throw a "hawk" (tomahawk), start a fire with flint and steel, make char cloth in a can in the fire (a fire starter), sew birch bark baskets, and weave porcupine quills to make bracelets. What was especially valuable here was that our host was not pretending. These skills were handed down to him from his ancestors. It was his culture. He shared his own past and history with us, allowing us to hear a more authentic voice, one that we couldn't experience had we simply read a book about Native American history.

In the evening, the park director and his wife sat around our fire and told stories as the Ojibwa and the fur traders did at the post long ago. They shared accounts from historic journals, of fistfights among the frightened fur traders, how they locked themselves inside the palisades when attacked and how they piled into their canoes and departed down the Yellow River in great haste while the village and post was burned to the ground.

Our children's interest in the fur-trading rendezvous era began years back when they first attended the local Long Rifle Rendezvous with Todd's aunt and uncle. Learning through history, particularly living history, is one of the richest and most lasting ways to get knowledge to stick. It's especially rewarding when children can incorporate what they've learned into their own personal life.

BRINGING THE LEARNING HOME

Sierra and Bryce were walking up nearby Hawk Mountain when they witnessed a road-killed rattlesnake. They already knew snakes play a vital role in the circle of life and do much to keep the mouse and rat population in check on a rural property. They knew the driver was ill-informed when, after she missed running over the snake on the road the first time, we watched as she threw her car into reverse and ran her tires over the snake the second time. She poked her head out the window and gleefully yelled, "Got it!" After Sierra and Bryce got over the unjust act of this ill-informed woman, Sierra wrote:

> *I thought back to the rendezvous we had attended months before and I remembered people talking about tanning snake hides. I thought it be something cool to try so I talked my dad into wading through the weeds to retrieve the snake. Back home, we dumped it in the freezer until we were ready to continue.*
>
> *My mom phoned a company that made a product called Snaketan, and we ordered a bottle after chatting with the amiable man, and he offered to ship out some color-coded snake anatomy print-outs for our dissection 'class.'*
>
> *It was an amazing experience to dissect such a large creature, especially a reptile. Since timber rattlesnakes are threatened in many places, most people do not get this opportunity. It was awesome to make comparisons on the parts of its body: the gall bladder, pancreas, kidneys, to ours. Even though it was a snake, it is amazing how much we share.*

This is a very good example of the reciprocal process of experiential education, where the experience inspires more reading, and research, and as a result, creates new experiences—and the cycle continues.

Taking the kids to organized public events like rendezvous and living history festivals inspired our family to put on our own celebrations that involved some form of living history and learning. This manifested itself in the form of alternate celebrations, particularly summer solstice parties. Getting together with family and friends was a goal, but the bigger goal was putting into practice some of the things that the kids had learned throughout that year, many gleaned from these living history events.

The parties had themes. One year, after visiting and participating in the Pennsylvania Renaissance Faire, a medieval summer solstice party was planned. Our family did research on costumes of the period, hunting secondhand stores and even sewing outfits, and we encouraged all attendees to embrace the time period too. We researched games that would have been played, like caper and hay bale toss and tug of war on a hemp rope, and planned our own competitions in the orchard. We researched food and planned a menu of items like roasted turkey legs and wine made with honey, and everyone ate by candlelight with only their hands and a knife.

Another summer was a Native American summer solstice party. We borrowed a twenty-four-foot Plains Indian canvas tipi and set it up in the orchard. We hunted for watercress and made salad seasoned with vinegar and honey. We harvested stag-horn sumac and boiled the red berries to make "pink lemonade." We dug a hole in the woods, wrapped freshly caught trout in skunk cabbage leaves, and roasted them in the ground. Todd taught the kids to start a fire with a bow drill and make drums out of deer hides that we had butchered. We danced around the fire while we shook homemade percussion instruments and played Native American flute music. The kids gave lessons on throwing atlatls, a primitive spear used by native people that they learned about at another festival.

All these events were inspired by the festivals and outings our children had attended as part of their experiential education. This was a very important part of their education, to not just witness and even participate in, but to recreate it themselves. This took their learning to an even deeper level. The summer solstice parties were a brilliant way to put into practice what they had learned and take on the role of educator themselves.

LIVING HISTORY MUSEUMS

If your family cannot take the time to participate in living history, the next best thing may be vacationing at two of America's quintessential living history "museums": Williamsburg in Virginia and the Plymouth Plantation in Massachusetts. Colonial Williamsburg was created from an actual town. Once visitors pass through the entrance, they are transported back in time to when Williamsburg was Virginia's colonial capital. Not only do the actors dress in authentic clothing, they speak and work in the style and the manner of the era, even using colonial diction and grammar. The three-hundred-acre town showcases eighty-eight original eighteenth-century buildings.

Plymouth Plantation depicts the history of Plymouth Colony. In the 1627 English Village section, first person interpreters have been trained to not just speak, act, and dress appropriately for the period, but also to remain in character and become "confused" if the visitors speak of anything from modern times. They speak in first person, answering questions and discussing their characters' lives and viewpoints while performing traditional jobs like tailoring, woodworking, and tinsmithing. They provide a lens into how our ancestors not only lived but how they thought and felt as well. These open-air museums are the closest thing to time travel that we can get. Their goal is to feed the human spirit by sharing America's enduring story. Williamsburg's motto, "The future may learn from the past," is something parents might take to heart when it comes to providing our children with the best education possible.

When our family attended events at the historic sites in Pennsylvania, we repeatedly encountered educator and living history actor Rich Pawling, of *History Alive!* Pawling takes characters that lived long ago and both entertains and educates during his first-person dramatizations. You might find him portraying a Conestoga wagoner, iron maker, abolitionist, canal man, railroad worker, wood-hick/logger, or an Irish coal miner. His authentic costumes and mannerisms are loud and boisterous, full of tobacco spitting and swearing, with period-accurate accents and vocabulary. His method of teaching the general public about these historic characters is hugely effective.

We were captivated by Pawling and often followed him to events. Years later, as a homeschooler in the eleventh grade, Sierra enrolled in the Human Geography course Pawling taught at Penn State University. Bryce and I often audited classes when Pawling pulled in his wagon of props and costumes, transporting his students back to a bygone era. The genius of Professor Pawling was the way he could educate different audiences in different spaces. He spanned the divide between public school/traditional education and his on-site living history reenactments for the general public.

He taught that "history is not merely a chronological record of events that took place with no relevance to us today. History starts coming alive when you realize it is people that make history, not dry facts in a textbook. By looking at the past, we can learn more about both who we are in the present, and where we are going in the future."

One of the side benefits of raising kids involved in living history is that a paradigm shift in their thinking can occur. According to Pawling, they are shown so many vivid examples of "what happened back then and what is now because of it," that they are able to connect dots and understand the universal law of cause and effect. The thought process of, in Pawling's words, "if you do this, this can occur" can perhaps help them be the wiser for it.

As a parent, it is sometimes difficult to get kids to think about their future. They might do thoughtless and dangerous things because they don't think it will have an impact on them down the road. It is good to think about and adopt the Seventh Generation Principle of Native American cultures. It is based on the Iroquois philosophy that we should consider seven generations into the future when it comes to making decisions, for what we do today impacts the future. We need to think and ask ourselves if this is going to be a good or a bad choice down the road? If we can become more knowledgeable about history, humankind might stand a better chance of not making the same mistakes again. No other way to learn has the possibility to reap this kind of insight and wisdom.

Another thought process that can result from learning about history is believing that you have an active part in what happens in your future. You have a choice, to a great extent, as to what path you decide on. This is hugely empowering and the sooner our children realize and accept the fact that they are most responsible for their future lives, they will make wiser, more thought-out choices to become who they want to be. They have all these examples from history to learn from. Children need vivid examples of people from the past who have followed their dreams, no matter how foolish sounding at the time. Learning history will help them to think beyond the present, into the future. Our children are standing on the shoulders of those who came before them. Standing there, they can see further.

NUTS AND BOLTS

Entire families can participate in reenactments. You may choose a historical character and do the research, reading biographies and other sources to portray the character as honestly and fully as possible. Researching a character also helps one see how individuals were embedded into and shaped by their historical contexts (politics, economics, social relations, livelihoods).

Keep your radar on for events where living history is brought to life. In the east, there are multiple Civil War encampments as well as many history-related events to attend. In the west, you have rich mining, and in the midwest, the westward expansion to explore. Use the area's Chamber and Visitor's Bureaus (CVBs) to locate events. State welcome centers offer tremendous amounts of materials and pamphlets where historical experiences (of any kind) can be gleaned. I visit my own welcome centers periodically just to see what new businesses or festivals have begun that I might not be aware of. Calendars of events in regional magazines are also good places to find experiences. Seek out opportunities where you can be involved as a participant instead of just observing, which will elevate the experience.

As children grow older, try to plan experiential learning trips that speak to their individual interests and needs. When our kids were teens, we traveled to the Finger Lakes region of New York for a weeklong exploration of the Underground Railroad and Women's Suffrage, visiting Harriet Tubman's and Susan B. Anthony's home, Seneca Falls, and the Women's Rights Historical Sites. We traveled to Massachusetts to discover Henry David Thoreau's cabin on Walden Pond, enjoy a swim in it, visit Ralph Waldo Emerson's house, and attend the Unitarian Church where he preached. In Wisconsin, we secured a houseboat on the Mississippi River and spent multiple days traveling downstream, negotiating the locks, talking to barge captains, learning how to captain a boat on this busy, historic river, all the while reading Mark Twain's *My Life on the Mississippi* to bring the experience to life. All these trips could be planned as part of a family vacation.

Besides America's National Historic Trails, there are other historic routes, like the 440-mile Natchez Trace Parkway in Tennessee, Alabama, and Mississippi and the 350-mile Erie Canalway Trail, both of which cater to cyclists. Besides a good bike ride, there are museums, historic sites, lock houses and preserved canal boats, to name just a few trailside attractions, combining history and outdoor recreation for your family.

CHAPTER 3

Learning from International Travel

"You have brains in your head. You have feet in your shoes. You can steer yourself any direction you choose."
Dr. Seuss, *Oh the Places You'll Go!*

CZECH REPUBLIC

I met tall Lubomir Chemelar, with his narrow, debonair mustache and slicked-back hair at an inn on Vermont's Long Trail. I was doing research for a magazine story I was writing on hiking inn to inn as a family; Lubomir was conducting his own research on what Americans were looking for in a rural lodging experience. He was in the beginning stages of creating a 250-mile greenway in his homeland that would travel from Vienna, Austria, to Prague, Czech Republic, called The Czech Greenway. We met over a cup of tea in the inn's kitchen late at night. "Perhaps we will work together some day," he said as he handed me his calling card.

I thought nothing of it. Our family was being seriously challenged at the Vermont B&Bs we were staying at. When we returned after a long day on the trail, four-year-old Sierra and two-year-old Bryce were exhausted and just wanted to quickly eat and go to bed. Instead, they had to wait patiently until 7 p.m. and sit quietly over multiple courses. It was a lot to ask of small children. International travel seemed far beyond our capabilities.

On New Year's Day of the next year, Todd was helping me clean off my desk and organize when we came across Lubomir's card. Todd was ready to toss it into the cylindrical file when I grabbed it and said, "Let me give ol' Lubomir a call."

Sure enough, Lubomir not only remembered me but invited our whole family to come to the Czech Republic that May. All expenses would be paid for the entire three weeks, in hopes of getting some press coverage back in the States. The greenway route followed the one-hundred-year-old trails built by the Czech Hiking Club traveling through twelve rural towns, the majority of which lie along medieval Moravia and Bohemia. We would be the guests of a nonprofit organization called the Friends of the Czech Greenway. The trip included other media folks, as well as tour operators hoping to package the excursion in the future. Todd and I had the only children.

Most young parents are pretty much consumed with just trying to get their children to bed at a decent time and eat healthy food. At this point in our lives, Todd and I were also trying to accomplish the Herculean task of getting Sierra and Bryce across the Continental Divide every summer as we made our way toward Mexico. An international trip on top of that, in the same calendar year, seemed a little daunting, but it was hard to turn down such an opportunity.

Travel abroad for my family growing up consisted of crossing over to the Canadian side at Niagara Falls; the same for Todd. Before our Czech Republic trip, we did not even own passports. Todd and I were convinced, however, that international, cross-cultural travel with a family would be a great way to learn. We believed it would increase our children's global awareness and stimulate their curiosity for the big world. A curious person is able to see new worlds and possibilities, move beyond the obvious and below the surface. International travel had the ability to increase one's appreciation for new and different viewpoints as well as for one's own culture, values that could not occur if our family remained in our comfortable, familiar life at home.

When Lubomir met Todd and me at the airport, with our children in tow, his first comment was, "This is crazy. I am crazy for bringing you poor people here." That made Todd and me uncomfortable, and it should have been a red flag. Then we saw the first few days' itinerary—a forty-two-mile bike ride, followed by a twenty-four-mile hike, then another forty-mile bike ride. Our concerns multiplied like the designated miles. Lubomir and his colleagues literally threw the itinerary together the day before the trip began, and it was obvious that they knew nothing about the capabilities of most hikers and cyclists, let alone a family with small children.

Our day started early. We ate breakfast at seven in the morning, yet we could not stop for lunch until late in the afternoon. We had to smuggle breakfast rolls loaded with apricot jelly wrapped in paper napkins to get the kids through the day, because there were no cafés or restaurants in the rural Czech countryside. When we hiked, we were made to walk ten miles without even a rest or a stop for a snack. Throughout a day of cycling, the kids could not get out of their trailer for hours, where they were crammed together in their bulky pile coats.

There were countless meetings with mayors and press conferences where we had to be present—the little American family promoting the Czech Greenway—and make the kids look happy on top of it. Of course, we did not understand a single word and the kids had to exercise extreme patience while the filming and interviews took place. Sierra finally broke down.

"I want to go home. I'm not having fun. I don't like it here. I can't understand what anyone is saying. I miss my kitties and my llamas. Either bring them here or I want to go to them."

Todd and I are not quitters. The adventuring philosophy we've adopted over the years is, "It may not always be easy, but it's always worthwhile." Unlike during our adventure in the Czech Republic, Sierra and Bryce did not need to force themselves to rally all those years llama packing on the Continental Divide Trail. Although that long trip certainly had its challenges, our family was in charge of decision making. Over the course of those five summers of hiking, the kids were pretty much always happy because Todd and I saw to it that their needs were met. Quitting and going home never entered the conversation. Such was not the case in the Czech Republic, at least at first.

Lubomir told us that we absolutely could not deviate from the itinerary, so Todd and I were forced to mutiny. My easy-going, usually timid husband assertively announced that we were going home. Part of this was a bluff tactic, so they understood the graveness of the situation and the need to find an alternative. The powers that be listened up, as they knew this was uncharacteristic behavior for Todd, and quickly accepted our terms. Todd and I examined the route every morning and evaluated the final destination. We then altered the itinerary to accommodate *our* family's ability and desire. None of the tour operators or media people in the group had been happy with the itinerary, either. Before long, everyone else in the group chose to follow our altered schedule. Todd and I ended up becoming consultants and the entire three-week trip turned completely around.

We learned one very important lesson on that Czech trip: When traveling with our young children, Todd and I needed to be in charge, not another leader or a tour operator. The Czech Republic trip was the first and the last led by someone other than ourselves.

Despite the initial challenges of the trip, the Czech Republic opened our eyes to the wonders of traveling to a foreign country. Our family developed a deep sense of curiosity for everything new, whether it was the land's beauty, the people's unusual customs, even their disturbing history. International travel took us way beyond our little bubble of life back home. It was a pivotal trip for us. It made us want to continue traveling for the rest of our lives.

Castles were a highlight, no matter what town we traveled to and each was unique in its own way. When we entered the wine cellar in Mikulov's castle, we marveled over one of the largest wine barrels in all of Europe, so immense that a person would have to drink three-and-a-half liters a day for eighty years to empty it. The kids were surprised to learn that many European countries drink wine like water—it is part of their culture. Even younger children, who would be considered under-age minors in America, are allowed to sip wine at meals.

We found wonder in the medieval town of Cesky Krumlov, as we dined inside the U Satlavy Restaurant, where all food was cooked over an open fireplace. Satlavy was a former medieval prison. It had stuccoed walls that reflected the warm candlelight, the only source of light in the eatery. Restaurant décor included prisoner's iron shackles still fastened to the walls.

We felt wonder over the Czech's strange menus, for when it came to food, my kids learned that vegetables "are for pigs." Our plate rarely included any more veggies than a tablespoon of corn or pickled cabbage. This was a far cry from how American parents are always harping at their children to "eat their vegetables."

The Castle Bitov, a fortress from the 1700s that clings to the precipice above Vranov Lake, was also a curiosity. A former owner of the castle, eccentric Baron Georg Haas, loved taxidermy and shared his collection with visitors: seventy-five stuffed dogs were arranged on the carpet of an elaborate parlor. He even had stuffed cats dressed in costumes and squirrels playing card games at tables and dancing the tango, which our kids found amazing.

While hiking one warm afternoon, we saw a middle-aged Czech woman, with well-endowed bosoms and a substantial belly roll, whip off her blouse and strip down to her white brassiere, simply because she was hot and uncomfortable. Sierra and Bryce looked on with gaping mouths. We told them that some Europeans have a different attitude towards modesty, even though her devil-may-care attitude was quite different from the puritan Germans who lived near us in Pennsylvania.

While pedaling through the medieval town of Telc, our children sang at the tops of their lungs. Window shutters were thrown open to see who was passing underneath: an American family on bicycles, pulling their small children in a trailer. The women in their babushkas hung over their open window sills, waving and smiling, and greeted us in Czech.

Curiosities in a foreign country can certainly include sadness, like war, the likes of which we do not attempt to shield our children from. These stores are part of the people's history and must be heard for an accurate picture. A large chunk of the Czech Greenway route consisted of traveling westward along the Czech-Austrian border. During the Communist regime, these lands were considered the end of the line, literally: the roads stopped in these well-preserved scenic towns. The people who lived there had not seen foreigners since the breakup of the Eastern Bloc, which was only five years before our visit. Some folks were so shy around strangers that they wouldn't even look us in the eye.

The wide green swath that was considered "no man's land" between the two countries, where vicious dogs had once roamed between the barbed wire and watch towers, still remained. Soldiers once stood with cocked rifles, we were told, ready to shoot Czechs who sought their freedom and made a run for it. Even children as young as five-year-old Sierra and three-year-old Bryce could hear a story of such oppression and feel empathy.

I have heard some people discuss the "perfect" age to take children traveling. There are even guidebooks discussing the exact recommended age for a trip to Disneyland. Todd and I believe that children are never too young to begin international travel. The positive effects may not surface until years later, but rest assured, children will be impacted. They will learn from the experience no matter the age. Parents, of course, are learning too, so you may as well as begin as early as possible and start to get good at it!

GOING BEYOND

After our Czech Republic trip, Todd and I realized that we knew enough to execute our own international family adventures. Being in charge and having the freedom to plan our own pace, rhythm, and style of travel made it that much easier. That first experience in the Czech Republic, however, gave us the confidence to make international travel a huge component in our children's upbringing and education. International travel teaches you about unpredictability, and unpredictability keeps life unceasingly interesting. Not that children have lived long enough in the world to become jaded or complacent or bored, but international travel probably does more to stave off those feelings in life than any other experience. If you show your curious children early on how big and varied the world is, traveling abroad can continue to be a constant source for entertainment, joy, and learning throughout their lives.

I did not know it then, but our Czech Republic trip was a key moment for me. This was when I became a family travel writer, an occupation that evolved into both a lifestyle and a job and an important tool by which we facilitated our children's education.

After we traveled to the Czech Republic, I decided that as a travel writer, I would not put my energy into creating solo travel opportunities. Instead, I decided to concentrate on creating international adventures for the entire family, and fly solo after the kids grew up and went off to college.

When the rare opportunity arose for me to travel solo, it was not met with approval from my children. When I announced that I was going on a trip to Cozumel with my girlfriends without the family, four-year-old Bryce fell apart.

While crying hard, my little actor flung himself on the sofa yelling, "I can't believe you're going away. At Easter! A holiday! I feel like I'm the boy in *Home Alone*. I can't believe you're going to leave me behind in this miserable life!"

I could barely contain myself from rolling with laughter, which he didn't appreciate, as he was dead serious. Sierra was also angry that she wasn't going. She hated to miss out on any adventure. I went without them to Cozumel, but after witnessing their drama, the children did not get left behind again. Perhaps Bryce's fit was enough to sway me to restructure my life. After that, international travel and culture quickly became a necessity in our children's lives.

Before we were set to take another international trip a few years later, we sought out creative ways to further immerse Sierra and Bryce in international culture without getting onto an airplane. When our library held a cultural evening, where half a dozen local folks who recently immigrated from foreign countries set up a booth at this public event. Dressed in their country's costumes, they offered ethnic foods to taste and a table full of craft items to handle, while their country's music played on a tape. Our family made friends with these folks who hailed from Lebanon, India, Pakistan, and China. We were invited to their homes to enjoy a meal, and even shared in the preparation so Sierra and Bryce could learn to cook a new dish. A local Indian family, the Singhs, encouraged us to visit the Vraj Hindu Temple to experience a worship service. This visit later sparked an interest in Sierra to peruse a project on world religions. Bryce became friendly with the Singhs' sons and was hired as a mentor by their mother to teach the boys a whole series of art lessons.

We attended summer ethnic festivals all over Pennsylvania (Polish, Greek, and Irish, among others), sampling their food, enjoying their music, and learning about the people and cultures who made our country what it is today. We took Sierra and Bryce to different ethnic restaurants—a Middle Eastern place, for example, which also show-cased belly-dancing on specific nights and offered an even greater feel for the culture of this part of the world. Todd and I sought out music concerts and performances, often held at local universities, like Andean pan pipe bands, Japanese drummers, and Irish step dancing, to continually feed our children's curiosity of the big world and its people.

SWITZERLAND

Our next big international trip after the Czech Republic was Switzerland, where my girlfriend Beth Ellen Pennell and her family were living and working for a few years. Sierra and Bryce were ten and eight years old at the time, and this trip focused primarily on hiking in the Swiss Alps, a sport we shared with this family. After exploring the area around Geneva, where the Pennells lived, and the neighboring French Alps, we headed to the south-central Oberland Heartland area.

Our family stretched ourselves in learning how to travel abroad. I had heard of an alternative, innovative travel company called Untours, whose slogan is "Independent travel with support." They placed our family in an apartment in a Swiss chalet, and gave us the opportunity to experience a foreign country and a culture at our own pace, free from the restrictions of scheduled tours. The best way to get to know a people and a culture is to live in that country, but since most of us do not have the luxury of time, we felt the next best thing was Untour. With them, we actually lived in a European community and saw Swiss life as insiders.

A group orientation was held the day we arrived in Oberland, along with other Untour American travelers. We learned the bus and train schedules, and how to find our way around the neighborhood. Our host and hostess, Heidi and Heinz Neiger, who lived downstairs from our apartment, spoke excellent English and helped us with hike planning.

Switzerland was a feast for our senses. In one day's hike, we witnessed a crashing avalanche and heard the voice of a native Swiss hiker who yodeled at the tops of his lungs as he walked along. Sierra and Bryce marveled at the beautiful Swiss brown cows that dotted the mountainsides and filled the air with the music of ringing bells. They were able to go up and pet a few heifers that looked like props in a spectacular movie set.

The most memorable day in Switzerland had to be our special visit to "Heidiland," in the town of Maienfield. (For the uninitiated: *Heidi* is a short novel about a five-year-old orphan girl who spends the summer with her grandfather high in the Swiss Alps tending goats.) Sierra and Bryce had read the book and seen the movie. They were thrilled to visit the quaint mountain town where the grandfather of author Johanna Spyri lived 130 years ago.

After our two-mile climb to the cabin, "Grandfather" carried a cutting board heaped with salt-cured slab bacon, homemade bread, and freshly made cheese to the rustic picnic table, and the children dug in, ravenous from our hike. This man was a retired postman, who actually tended to cows and goats on the mountain slopes. He was appointed by the town to help bring the children's classic to life for the boys and girls and their families who came every spring and summer from all over the world to walk in Heidi's footsteps.

This experience helped literature and film come alive for Sierra and Bryce; reading and viewing first, then actually going there in person to reach deeper levels of learning. Todd and I were able to execute these continued travels abroad because we took small, manageable steps, by first seeking out friends like the Pennells, who already resided in a foreign country and offered to host us; then signing up with a company like Untours. These stepping stones built our confidence and knowledge base to successfully travel abroad as a family.

CHINA

Before Sierra and Bryce went off to college, our family had visited a dozen countries. Most of those trips were for a month or longer, enabling us to immerse ourselves in the culture and learn as much as we could.

One of the most educational take-aways from all of this international travel was how our idea of what we think of as "normal," or even "good" can be challenged and then altered. Our personal lifestyle, belief systems, and behaviors makes complete sense to us, and to a large extent, even to our fellow Americans. Foreign customs can be drastically different from ours, yet they may make complete sense in context, and work beautifully. Traveling is the perfect way to stretch a person's acceptance and broaden their mind. It teaches us to live without judgement. No other country illustrated this to us more than China. Part of our surprise with what we found there had to do with our misconceptions—with what we *thought* we'd find before we arrived in country.

Our family went to China to visit Sierra, who, after college, was teaching English in Mianyang, in the Sichuan Province. In the month that we were in country, we traveled all around the province as well as to many other cities and national parks. But it was not the China we had imagined.

Appearance and image seemed hugely important to the Chinese people. Nearly all Chinese people in the cities were impeccably dressed. Women wore fancy high-heeled boots, short skirts with tights, and colorful winter jackets; the men mostly dressed in solid black. We didn't see a scuffed shoe in the entire month of travel. Their cities, as well, were immaculate. In our travels, we never saw a single piece of trash—not a straw or a cigarette butt or even a fallen leaf. Multitudes of Chinese people were employed as street sweepers, using grass brooms. We even saw women cleaning and polishing the guard rails on the super highways!

Contrary to this cleanliness philosophy, Chinese mothers had a surprisingly unusual way they allowed and encouraged their toddlers to move their bowels—wherever they wanted, whether it was as in a stylish shopping mall, or the historic Forbidden Palace. And not in a bathroom, but right on the floor. Some toddlers wear crotchless pants instead of diapers. They were bundled in winter jackets, hats and gloves, but their crotches were open to the elements. When they have to poo or pee, they either squat wherever they are, or their mothers suspend them in mid-air. The mother might lay a tissue on top, or not bother at all.

We saw a pile on the polished floor inside the airport terminal. When we walked, we did not look out for dog turds; we looked out for baby turds. This felt like a major contradiction to us.

Chinese air can be truly unbreathable. In the cities, everyone wore face masks. Because of the widespread respiratory sickness that plagues so many, everyone hacks up phlegm and spits constantly—everywhere—in the nicest restaurants, in trains, right on the floor. Since it is very cold in the winter, frozen globs of sputum are everywhere. Here seemed like another contradiction. Why was so much energy put into appearance in one area but tossed to the wind in another? We've since learned that the Chinese consider this mucous "toxic," and so getting it out of the body is a "healthy" activity and so they don't make a fuss about it, as well as blowing their noses indoors onto the floor.

We were cold the whole month we were in China. It was freezing inside many buildings, except for the finest hotels. There was no heat on for the entire month of winter that we visited. Inside schools and restaurants everyone wears down jackets, hats, and gloves. They don't just accept it; they go one step further and leave doors and windows hanging wide open to the twenty-degree weather while trying to enjoy a restaurant meal. We learned afterwards that in most places in China, heat is a government-run, public system, operated by public officials. There are massive central boilers that send out heat via hot-water radiators. It has to be "unreasonably cold" for heat to be turned on, and that concept, we discovered, is all relative.

Perhaps that is why the Chinese conducted so much of their lives out-of-doors, even in the winter, which is a stark contrast to American life where most run from heated house to heated car to heated office and store. They did not hide indoors like many Americans do, cranking our heat so high we need to strip down to T-shirts.

There were card games going on in the streets, women sat knitting, and me played mahjong. School recess was held outdoors in the winter months and ping-pong was the children's game of choice. There were dozens of ping-pong tables lined up in the school yards. On lunch break, business professionals in suits came out to the street to play badminton on the sidewalks. We climbed a hill in a park and someone stood alone in the woods just singing their heart out, or did tai chi or danced with a long scarf to music. On a stone square, an artist drew Chinese characters with water and a large brush as a way of meditation, for before long, the beautiful characters dried and disappeared. They embraced the cold, the winter, and continued with their lives outdoors regardless of how low the thermometer dipped.

Of all the things we found wonderfully strange and different, it was the food that left the most lasting impression, especially on Bryce.

Bryce wrote in his journal: *"I have always embraced the weird and bizarre, so I was fascinated to watch the young adults on the bus and train eating their favorite snack. They opened up the snack packages of boiled, pale chicken feet, and with their teeth, scraped off the skin and whatever miniscule meat was on them, concluding with spitting out the toenails. I did not partake but I did in Hot Pot, which I thoroughly enjoyed. We dipped duck feet, mini squid, and long intestines into the boiling fat with our chopsticks. I did draw the line, however, at the man selling skinned dogs from the handlebars of his bicycle, and passed on the sheep testicles in our dinner in the Tibetan highlands."*

Our misunderstandings of and fascination with Chinese culture proved to be a two-way street. How they viewed our American western culture or what they choose to adopt was equally as puzzling. For example, in the school where Sierra taught, the students and the teachers took on English words as names, such as Immaculate, Warcraft, Mole, God, Death, Crucifix, Cancer, Aroma, Martini, Beyond, Coffee, and a teacher called Mr. Horse. They showed little interest in what the words actually meant, but cared more for how the word sounded when they pronounced it, which seemed so strange to us.

China was a curiosity. We spent most of our time there being amazed, and our heads constantly full of questions. Out of the fifty countries I have personally traveled to, it stands above the rest in that respect. It helps with understanding if the traveler can ask the local folk questions, research to learn more, delve into the "why" of some behavior or custom. We did some of this during and after our trip to China but could have used more. But our take-away was realizing that one of the greatest gifts of traveling to China, or anywhere in the world, was how high it raises the bar for inflaming curiosity. A curious mind is stimulated to learn, dig deeper to understand, and find a place of commonality. A visit to a foreign country is a colossal learning experience that can be satisfied no other way.

NUTS AND BOLTS

HOW CAN WE AFFORD TO TRAVEL ABROAD?

People may get the idea, from the way we travel, that Todd and I are wealthy. But nothing could be further from the truth. Our simple lifestyle at home rewards us with many gifts but also some disposable income, even though our occupations do not generate substantial money. Gathering experiences and learning from them was where Todd and I put our energy and what residual income we generated.

Before 9/11, there were excessive dollars available for tourism sponsorship. International travel writing was thriving and I was a self-proclaimed advocate for family travel. I could sell a front-page, full-color travel feature to nearly any major newspaper. As a result, a few countries found the funds to bring my entire family abroad and foot the bill. That opportunity did not last many years, however, and my family was forced to learn to travel on a meager budget.

In our everyday life at home, we never purchased anything that we did not absolutely need, rarely ate out, and saved all our excess money for travel. I began to use my credit card to rack up airline miles. I used it for nearly every purchase made throughout the year—a year's worth of health insurance, auto and homeowners insurance, and the first five thousand dollars on a vehicle purchase. We paid off our cards every month, using our savings account money, and were never charged interest. I was able to secure flights for all four of us to Alaska, Hawaii, then Mexico's Yucatan Peninsula with frequent-flyer points. If I had to purchase flights, I did so far in advance, so they were cheaper and my bank account could recover and build the funds back up for when we arrived in the country.

Once there, we traveled cheaply. We often powered ourselves on bikes, as in Ireland, where we pedaled right out of the Shannon airport on our tandems, then circled the island for five weeks. We tackled the five-hundred-mile Camino de Santiago (The Way of Saint James) in Spain on our bikes as well. And did a three-week cycling tour of Mexico's Yucatan Peninsula. This kept transportation costs low but also connected our family intimately to the land and the people. We were not insulated in a private rental car but were able to talk to locals, stop more frequently, and be open to serendipitous adventures. If we did not cycle, we often used public transportation as in Patagonia and Sicily, where we got around by bus.

We traveled like the locals, and we ate where they ate. We purchased food at grocery stores and markets, fixed simple meals of bread and cheese, ate street food from vendors (with caution) and at neighborhood cafés where the local people ate, which kept the food experience authentic. We camped whenever we could (we were even able to find a campground in Rome) or stayed at international youth hostels or very inexpensive hotels. It was a sacrifice that we made in order to stay in a country longer. We found that a good month in each country was necessary in order to see the land, learn who its people were, and gather enough experiences to make those four flights worth it.

Our family of four was often able to travel for an entire month on just a few thousand dollars. We chose countries where it was very inexpensive to live, such as Thailand or Nepal, even if flights there were pricey.

Todd and I learned this Spartan-like lifestyle as long-distance backpackers. We all had our initial traveling experiences out on the trail in the wilderness, so our comfort bar was much lower than the average traveler's. Our children also had no problem whatsoever traveling like this.

Because of these "sacrifices," our family was able to travel and use the whole world to learn. It became our classroom. There were challenges and obstacles, of course. We learned that right from the get-go in the Czech Republic, but there was nothing we couldn't learn to work around, including our public school.

DEALING WITH THE SCHOOL ADMINISTRATION

When Sierra and Bryce attended public school, which they did for seven years, they habitually missed school every September. They not only used up their five allowed field trip days the very first week, but continued to stay out for weeks more. It was our family's favorite time to travel. Christmas break was another good time to plan a trip, usually to a warmer climate. Sierra and Bryce often missed another whole month around the holidays, and they were out over Easter break, Thanksgiving, and the end of the school year. I took advantage of these few designated days off and extended them into full-blown adventures. In between these long trips, we incorporated many smaller ones.

I was upfront with the school administration right from the start and did not try to sneak around the rules, nor deceive them. I delivered my speech of how adventure travel writing is my occupation and since I specialized in family travel, I needed my children with me. I guaranteed that the children's schoolwork would accompany them and they would be kept up to speed with their classmates. The administration was unbelievably supportive.

Their middle school principal said the following to Todd and me at a parent-teacher conference: "There are rules that are set in place in education for most of the students, but there are shades of gray. What you do with your children is not for everyone. A child has to be highly motivated to conduct this type of alternative education successfully. Your children want to go on these trips because they care about their education, because they want to learn. It is not a vacation for them. I know what you are doing with your children is very good for them. I know this lifestyle is the best for them and that is all I care about."

It was a huge gift to have allies in the administration. It made our job as our children's alt-educators so much easier. Todd and I saw no limits to where we might travel to, and no reason to keep them in school any more than we had to. We felt as though we had been given free reign with no boundaries. Travel and experiential learning on the road had become a cornerstone in our children's education curriculum. We gave them the best of both worlds: an adventurous, traveling life that taught huge lessons that could not be learned in the classroom, as well as some socializing and a great variety of instructors at their public school.

Sierra and Bryce always took their schoolwork with them on a trip in the form of copied pages and worksheets, although Todd and I thought it important to not get bogged down with busy work when they were trying to immerse themselves in a culture and a place. When we were in Cozumel and the night square filled with local families playing music and creating artwork and the children running and playing, Sierra was up in the hotel room doing Spanish worksheets. I forced her to stop and mingle with the people, and practice her Spanish conversation skills.

For half a dozen years, our family went about with this yo-yo type of lifestyle, pulling the kids out of school for multiple trips during the school year, both short and long term, both local and international. Sierra and Bryce did not enjoy taking all the make-up tests once they returned to school and it was challenging to continually transition back and forth. They experienced some anxiety associated with constant change, but they were able to adapt, at least in elementary school. By the time Sierra was in middle school, however, she had had enough. Todd and I were persuaded to pull them out of public school and allow them to teach themselves. They would be responsible for their own education. I would be their facilitator. Sierra spent her last four years being in charge of her education and Bryce six years. There was absolutely no time constraint to our travel after this.

THE STEPS TO MAKE IT HAPPEN

What are the steps that we took to plan and execute a trip abroad? We got destination ideas from websites, by typing in searches like "family friendly destinations" and "budget travel/affordable places." We read travel magazines and got ideas from articles. We talked to friends and acquaintances about their travel experiences. Once we had a few ideas, we searched Google flights, looking for particularly inexpensive destinations. The costs may depend on which countries are currently investing in tourism and attempting to attract travelers. Going off season or during shoulder seasons can also reap considerable discounts.

We purchased used guidebooks from Amazon for a penny plus postage and visited discount stores where last year's travel guides are greatly reduced. We read them for ideas of what is available in a particular country, but before we left on a trip, we made sure we purchased the latest edition of the guidebook, and certainly more than one publisher's. Our go-to guides had always been Lonely Planet and Moon for the most alternative, budget-minded travel tips.

We kept in touch with folks that we met from other countries and developed friendships with them. We opened our home to foreigners, sharing our way of life, and they often invited us to come visit them in their country. This way of extending ourselves and our home to other people was natural for us.

Working with tourism offices is also a good place to seek information and ask for advice. I personally liked to converse on the phone. The tourism offices I called in the United States often went on to connect me to their offices abroad, after they personally made the initial query on our family's behalf. The in-country expert could then deliver specific travel assistance tailored to our family's individual needs, such as helping to secure reservations and build itineraries where there might be an in-country language challenge.

Multiple times, I have approached tour operators and enlisted their help in setting up an independent trip for our family, for a fee. Although we did not want to go on their planned group trips, the operators possessed the expertise and contacts to help our family craft our own trip. We successfully did this in the Yucatan Peninsula with a cycling company, EcoColors Tours. They set up our two-week trip for us, making all our reservations ahead of time, and helped us store our extra traveling gear and bike shipping boxes while we were on our trip.

I often set up accommodations on websites like www.booking.com and www.hostelworld.com and secured reservations before we left. We also did this en route, but sometimes, with a family, it was nice to have less to deal with in country. There are enough uncertainties when traveling with children that leaving everything up to chance at the last minute can be asking for too much. At the very least, I made the most important reservations before we left home.

CHAPTER 4

Learning about Values and Priorities

"The world's much smaller than you think. Made up of two kinds of people—simple and complicated. The simple ones are contented. The complicated ones aren't."

Margaret Moore, *Willie Without*

NAVAJO RESERVATION

Hot oil sizzled in the pan as I kneaded the fry bread dough. My new Navajo friend, Rose, stood closely, instructing me. Outside the old trailer, her eight children joined ours in a game of hide-and-seek, a universal game that crosses all language barriers. (Although Navajo children learn English once they go to school, Navajo is the preferred language among all ages.) I told my children to watch out for the barbed-wire clothesline that hung dangerously at eye level. An American flag flapped in the breeze from a tin shelter hung there to welcome us, they told us.

My family was cycling New Mexico's Great Divide Mountain Bike Trail for 650 miles through this arid state. One hundred miles of it passes through the Navajo's private property. We knew we would be trespassing when we got off the road to camp at night and the open country did not allow us to inconspicuously set up camp, as we normally did on public lands. Fortunately, we had met Rose at the post office and she invited us back to her home for the night.

I snatched glances around the house as we cooked. I saw broken screen doors, duct-taped windows, and Scotch-taped countertops. I felt self-conscious about my apparent wealth, our ability to cut out of regular life and pursue this multi-month adventure, even though this was my "job" in a great sense. I longed to point out that back home, we live rather simply and, especially on the trail, that we may have more commonalities than differences. Perhaps she already sensed this, or she would not have reached out to us.

As we made bread together, Rose told me that many Navajo still practice the old ways, despite religious groups who have come in to establish churches and teach them "a better way." Some still live in hogans, a traditional, small round hut, take sweat baths, and hold dances for the sick, and there are medicine women that still practice.

When the sun went down, Rose took me on a walk to her favorite lookout point. We passed her relatives' broken-down trailers and modular homes. She recalled matter-of-factly a brother who abandoned his family, a sister-in-law who is in jail, a young boy who had just been murdered in a fight. Poverty, alcoholism, and unemployment defined much of her family's life. In the same breath Rose proudly pointed out sacred peaks, sandstone cliffs, pastel bluffs, all radiating beautiful color in this evening light. The Navajo are rich in magnificent country. Rose understood how these two realities of Navajo life are integrated and cannot be separated. We both could appreciate the beauty yet, at the same time, acknowledge the pain.

I was moved that she trusted me enough to open up and share such personal information. I wondered if it was because of our mode of transportation—bikes—and being in the company of our children. Cycling is a slower way to move across the land. It creates opportunities to connect to people. As they opened up and shared their lives, true understanding and education began.

As we loaded up our bikes the next day, Rose sorted through her children's things for presents: an oversized blouse for Sierra, a broken toy for Bryce. Perhaps she wanted to give us a parting gift to remember them by. Our whole family was quiet after this potlatch, for we were bombarded with emotions and tried to make sense of them.

Even though our material things had been pared down to the basic essentials on this bike trip, it became clear to us how wealthy we were next to our new friends and how privileged we were to be able to partake in a long-distance cycling trip. In my mind, however, it was our encounter with this Navajo family that really made us rich, not the high-end tandem mountain bikes we had received from a manufacturer in exchange for writing about our experience. We all acquired a new reference point for wealth, even my six-year-old, as we headed out across the reservation road. Our Navajo visit was the topic of choice for many miles of pumping pedals.

Our kids' questions were simply, "What exactly is poverty?" and "Are we poor?"

This experience on the Navajo reservation laid the groundwork for our children's understanding of the difference between a need and a want. I explained that I not only find something like designer sneakers and clothing impractical and mainly a status symbol, but we as a family make a conscious choice to spend less on material items so we will have more money to spend on travel adventures like this bike trip.

They got that. Children catch on fast if you take the time to talk and explain to them. Material things their peers deem necessary in order to be happy (or accepted) never appeared on their Christmas lists. Life on the trail showed them how few material things are actually needed in life in order to be happy and exposed them to what true poverty is at a remarkably young age.

This lifestyle choice went back to our early years when Todd and I spent many months living in the wilderness as long-distance backpackers. On the trail, we needed nothing more than what we carried in our packs. We had our bed (sleeping bag and pad), our home (tent), our kitchen (small cook-kit and tiny gasoline stove), and our clothing that fit into a small stuff sack. Our mode of transportation was our boots and our feet. Walking for months at a time gave us the gift of freedom and independence and turned these values into a requirement for our happiness. Life was distilled down to the simple act of walking in profound beauty. Our bodies became amazingly strong and our heads clear. We saw that many of the material trappings of the modern world, which were absent in the woods, like expensive cars, large homes, lots of adult toys did not contribute to our happiness, but quite the opposite. Acquiring them would necessitate becoming a slave to generating money to purchase and maintain them. As a result of this minimalist lifestyle, our needs in life became few and simple.

Todd and I determined very early in our life together that we could either figure out a way to make more money or figure out a way to need less. We acquired skills, which fostered independence, and worked at occupations in which we were in control of our time. We designed a simple lifestyle where we did not need a hefty income and were not buried under debt. We followed the philosophy made famous during World War II, "Use it up, wear it out, make it do or do without." In times of abundance, we squirreled money away in the bank; during lean times, we withdrew. We lived within our means. Embracing voluntary simplicity was not the philosophy that most conventional Americans lived by. But Todd and I were following our hearts when it came to our lifestyle choice and our priorities. This philosophy spread to how we raised and educated our children.

A few years after our bike ride through Navajo land, Todd and I were contemplating whether to take the family to Thailand for a month to visit a very close friend who invited us to her home in Chiang Mai. During this period, while Sierra was sitting on our living room sofa, she discovered that if she pounded the pillow, a cloud of disintegrated foam dust puffed from the fabric. The sofa had been around for a long time. I inherited it after my parents both died and we split up the home's contents.

Sierra questioned me, "Don't you think we need a new sofa?"

"We could buy one," I told her. "Or we could save that money and use it to go to Thailand where you can ride an elephant through the Hill Tribe country and sea kayak with monkeys."

"I think the sofa is just fine," she immediately decided, not missing a beat.

We did not "need" the trip to Thailand or the new sofa. Both were wants. It came down to what our family valued most, where our priorities lay. We chose to make do in one area in order to free up money in another area. Experiences rather than things were what brought our family the most joy.

Dr. Thomas Gilovich, a psychology professor at Cornell University, has studied the question of money and happiness for two decades. "Our experiences are a bigger part of ourselves than our material goods," says Gilovich. "You can really like your material stuff. You can even think that part of your identity is connected to those things, but nonetheless they remain separate from you. In contrast, your experiences really are part of you. We are the sum total of our experiences." As Sierra and Bryce grew up, it became obvious that their identity was clearly growing out of their experiences.

THAILAND

The sound of muffled pounding woke us from our sleep. A tiny fire illuminated the workplace of the thirteen-year-old Thai girl who was pounding rice for the day's meals. Her muscular leg stomped down on the log beam that caused a mortar to strike a deep bowl containing unhulled rice. She had to do this chore every day for an hour, in order to reap about two quarts of rice. To our family, this seemed like very hard work for a teenager, but our guide told us on our tour of this hill tribe village that she was just married and had a long life of hard work ahead of her. This fact amazed eleven-year-old Sierra, who was finding the culture of Thailand a world apart from her life in Pennsylvania. Living in this village, Sierra would only have two more years of freedom and childhood play before becoming a woman, a wife, a mother. This sobering fact occupied her mind for a long time.

Our family went on this month-long adventure to Thailand four years after we cycled through New Mexico. A local friend, Susan McCartney, had moved there on business with her husband and invited our family to come for a visit. Although Thailand was not on our travel radar, it quickly moved to the top.

When the elephants with the heavy chains around their necks and feet arrived at our hut a few hours later, I had to throw fear to the wind. The *mahout*, or elephant driver, with a cloth wrapped loosely around his head, the tattoos up and down his arms and rolled-up smoking leaves between his teeth, made eye contact with me and motioned for Bryce. He wanted me to lift my ten-year-old son up over the elephant's head and put him in the basket behind him. We were off for a half-day ride through the jungle.

The mahout bounced on the elephant's neck and sang to her in an eerie chant the entire time he drove. The elephant's baby followed close behind and we occasionally stopped for her to nurse. We rocked and swayed with the animal's large purposeful steps. The big leathery ears flapped back and forth across our lower legs while our feet rested on the animal's great head like a footstool. Orchids hung from the trees and were easily visible at this height. The mahout turned around and with his stained and missing teeth, smiled at us. He took my son from the basket and placed him on the elephant's head in front of him. Bryce turned around and beamed at me and I knew then I made the right decision to bring my family to this country.

As we entered the Karen village along the Mae Klong River on our elephants, a young girl was fishing, a man was kneading soapy laundry on a flattened log, and a pig was rooting in the mud—normal village goings-on. We walked around the village, watching the pigs and chickens that roamed freely and lived under the huts on stilts, eager to snag any scrap of food that fell through the bamboo floors. Families cooked supper on open fires, women sat nursing babies, embroidering cloth, winnowing rice.

In an open dirt lot, some children were batting a plastic bottle over a badminton net. With no rackets or birdie, they used the next best thing. My kids joined in and discovered that a language barrier is nonexistent when it comes to laughter. They also understood that you can make do with whatever "toy" is available, and having fun has more to do with a state of mind than any material object.

We had been told before we left the states that the Hill Tribe children are very poor, so we should pack up any outgrown sweaters or long pants in a backpack and bring them along to distribute. Our friend Susan located a family shivering in the forty-degree evening air. They stood in line and each claimed an article. Throughout our visit to the village, my kids continued to recognize their clothing on children playing. Susan told them that each article would be valued and passed down for many more years. Although my children were not new to the secondhand/ recycled clothing philosophy, it was a new realization—how valuable even used clothing could be. Normally, their outgrown clothing is just bagged up and sent to Goodwill without a second thought. To think their hand-me-downs will get passed on and on for decades until they become rags, making many children happy here in this place so far from home, was a very heartwarming thought.

I once read an article in a women's magazine about a mother who was facing challenges with her pubescent-age child. She recommended taking them to a developing country at this point so that they can understand how very much we have in America. They then would come to understand that they and their "needs," like the latest iPhone and designer clothing, are in reality perceived needs. Traveling to developing countries clearly illustrates this distinction and does much to align our priorities. Although I did not bring my children to Thailand (or the Navajo Nation) with this solely in mind, we saw examples of what is necessary in order to survive and what are just extras, over and over again, and that the state of happiness has little to do with how many material objects we possess, but a state of mind. Experiences like these reinforce the belief that we should live with a profound sense of gratitude for what we have and not take things for granted.

THE YUCATAN

When Todd and I were looking for a place for our family to cycle on a long-distance adventure over the winter months, Mexico's Yucatan Peninsula ranked high on the destination list. Much of the Yucatan is considered safe for families and has gentle weather in the winter. The terrain is flat and easy, and there is a myriad of extra activities to break up the ride and make the trip more fun. Traveling by bicycle is a great way to go in developing countries because this simple mode of transportation connects you to the native peoples on an intimate, less intimidating level. They all cycle themselves and are very receptive to cyclists.

On our two-week trip, each day we cycled a half day to a new destination, then snorkeled, swam with sea turtles, caved, and visited the Mayan ruins of the Yucatan. Besides a side trip to an island or two like Cozumel, our main cycling tour was along the exquisitely beautiful Riviera Mayan coast, from Cancun to Tulum, a 100-mile strip. We then left the shore and headed inland to the ruins of Coba and Chichen Itza, finishing with a jaunt up north to see the pink flamingo preserves.

We avoided the busy roads with no shoulders and selected routes through tiny villages. We opted to eat where the locals eat—at tiny, open-air, no-nonsense restaurants where we sat on cheap, plastic, stackable chairs and no one spoke a word of English. But the food was authentic, cheap, and delicious. The owners were always surprised and happy to see courageous gringos out of their element.

We passed stick homes with thatched grass roofs, with no doors and windows, just the open air with weather passing through. Catching a glimpse inside the rooms as we passed, we saw little furniture, but colorful, woven hammocks hung from the ceiling as beds. Smiling children ran out to the streets yelling "*Hola! Hola!*" as we cycled past. We yelled, "Ho-la!'" back and they all giggled as, I believe, we put the emphasis on the wrong syllable.

In the ancient Mayan city of Coba, our kids became friendly with José, a sixteen-year-old tricycle-taxi driver who led us around a huge network of white stone roads (*sacbes*) at the archeological site. On our tour, we stopped to climb the sacrificial monuments covered with moss, pulling ourselves up the very narrow, steep steps with a fat sisal rope. Thirteen-year-old Sierra wrote in her journal: *"I think how lucky I am. Most who climbed this tower did not get to go back down. Although it is hot and I am sweating, I shiver, thinking of the rivulets of blood that draped these white stones after heads were lopped off in sacrifice."*

Once we explored the historic site, José asked if we'd like to tour his village and see where he lives. Sierra wrote:

After José pedals us down to a rickety dock to show us their resident crocodile, he pedals us to the far side of the lake where he lives with all the other Mayan people. This is poor, very poor, and it reminds me of the hill villages of Thailand. José points out his house—a very simple bamboo slated shack with a thatched palm roof. "Is bad," he comments. My heart goes out to him, yet I'm enthralled by this strange way of life. He shouts greetings to his friends who ride by on their rusty gearless bikes like his own. He seems to know everyone, and his friends seem happy. I try to imagine myself living in his village. Could I be happy?

He pedals us to his school, where we peek into the poor, plaster-peeling walls and assorted old and scratched desks. Nonetheless,

Christmas garland decorates the bare, ugly walls. Outside in the courtyard, smiling girls with bare feet and tattered clothes count 'uno, dos, tres, cuatro, cinco, seis', as they learn the movements to a Mayan dance. On the concrete walls outside is a crude painting of clouds, rain, the ocean, and the sun connected by arrows. They must be learning about the water cycle.

That night, we invited José to join us for dinner, and over the meal he told my children how they only stay in school until the eighth grade. Although Spanish is spoken in the schools, at home, the ancient Mayan language is preferred. The kids had fun teaching one another how to say Mayan words and English words, laughing and getting to know this boy from another world.

Sierra concluded, *"As we walk back to our hotel, I think of my fellow classmates back in school, as they try to learn about the ancient Mayan people in textbooks, and here are their descendants, real Mayans, taking us around in their homeland. I have a lot to think about as I fall asleep and compare my life to José's."*

This encounter was very beneficial for my teenagers because José was a peer who willingly opened up and showed them his world. Connecting to a human being, hearing him speak about his life, was very personal and impacting compared to a tourist observing as he/she traveled about, always on the periphery. It was easy for Sierra and Bryce to make a parallel between his life and theirs, and examine how little these people had compared to most Americans and how little it has to do with happiness.

PENNSYLVANIA'S AMISH COUNTRY

There are stretches of road in parts of Lancaster County, Pennsylvania, where there are no phone or electric wires, just pure, unobstructed scenery. There are more horses and buggies traveling these rural roads than automobiles. Some people could look at the Amish and Old Order

Mennonites' lifestyle and see their lack of material things and simple living as a form of poverty, but it is not; it is a choice. They are rich in family, their God, and the miraculous land which sustains them. As we moved through their land on our bicycles, we felt as if we were slipping back in time, or moving into a foreign country, retreating from the life we'd known, and it felt good.

The Amish are descendants of the Anabaptists and adhere to a strict sixteenth-century sect that seeks a return to the simplicity of faith and practice of the early Christian church as depicted in the Bible. The Old Orders (as opposed to the more modern groups) drive horse-drawn carriages, dress "plain," refrain from using electricity, and emphasize occupations close to farm and home.

Inside the buggy windows, we saw women wearing dark-colored dresses with black bonnets tied under their chins while the men wore straw hats and wire-rimmed glasses. My children waved, and they responded with shy half-smiles. All along our ride were signs advertising the sale of their handicrafts and the fruits of their farms: quilts, wooden wagons, birdhouses, brown eggs, cheese, vegetables, and baked goods. Each of their spotless, well-kept farms added to the breathtaking scenery.

While visiting Amish country, our family chose to stay at working farm B&Bs owned and run by Mennonites so that our children could participate in caring for their animals at the end of the day's ride and we could all immerse ourselves a little deeper into their daily lives.

The Amish children were all barefoot; all had brown-stained foot soles and strong, healthy-looking bodies. A young girl rode her horse bareback through a creek, herding the cows home for their milking. An old Amish farmer led a sheep down the road on a leash with two others following closely behind. A few chickens ran across the small road and narrowly missed my front tire. We waved to men in the fields as they loaded bales of hay onto their wagon, and they waved back. Life is simple here in Amish country.

At a covered bridge, we took a break to catch minnows and let the kids slop in the creek. Amish children came by on their bikes and, for the first time, stopped to talk, asking about our bikes, something we all had in common. Our family rode on tandems for this tour, and the Amish kids had not seen such bikes before.

Traveling to all of these locations—New Mexico's Navajo Nation, Thailand's Hill Country, Mexico's Yucatan Peninsula, and Pennsylvania's Amish country—actually made Todd and I feel confident about the simple, low-consuming lifestyle that we have chosen to pursue and share with our children. These experiences clearly mapped out our values and priorities and gave Sierra and Bryce much fodder when adopting their own lifestyles in the future. We hoped that they would choose to live within their means when they grew up and would not become consumed with consuming.

NUTS AND BOLTS

If your family has hopes of incorporating more travel into its lifestyle, you have to consider that not every family member may share the same level of passion for the activity. Not everyone will rank travel high on their list of priorities. In our family, travel was seen as a definite need for Sierra, Bryce, and me; for Todd, not as much. During the children's formative years, Todd was The Trail Boss, leading his family down the Continental Divide. After that, he mostly took a back seat in our travels, as a mere follower, not a leader. The burden of planning a trip and leading the children around the planet rested almost entirely on my shoulders. When it came to leaving home, we often had our differences.

This difference in priorities was first brought to my attention when Sierra was only nine months old. Todd and I planned a one and a half month hiking and camping trip to the desert canyons of Utah. But when Todd realized that the trip coincided with the cabbage harvest, he said, "We can't go! We have to make sauerkraut!"

I told him I would gladly buy him a case of organic sauerkraut to compensate. We were not going to allow half a dozen heads of cabbage dictate our lives. That was the first in a long line of differences between the two of us on how we wanted to spend our time.

As the years went by, the kids and I became more and more addicted to travel, yet Todd felt home pulling stronger. He created a lifestyle on our property—in the garden, in the orchard, with our animals. With the construction of a fully equipped blacksmith forge as well as a complete woodworking shop, his longing to create often outweighed his need to see the world. He was often torn between deciding between the two, going and staying. I helped him make his decisions. As the kids grew older and easier to handle, Todd stayed home on domestic trips. On extended international trips, however, or adventures involving long-distance cycling and paddling, he came along and usually gladly. Once he got away from home and his projects and work, he forgot about them and got into the magic of the place. He did have his limits however, and three weeks, we discovered, was it. Not four weeks.

We were walking down the Great Wall of China, on our last week of our month-long trip, when the kids noticed that their father looked sullen, apathetic, and moody.

They asked, "What is wrong, Dad?"

"I'm ready to go home," he said.

They replied, "You're on the frickin' Great Wall of China, one of the Wonders of the World! Aren't you happy to be here?" and he replied, "I've had enough." And there we had it. Everyone has their limit, and it's important to be sensitive where we each draw that line.

Todd opened up the space that allowed us to educate Sierra and Bryce in the way that we saw fit. He brought in the majority of our family income and I was the chief education facilitator. One could not function healthfully without the other. It was a partnership. But it was important to be sensitive to what each of us valued and considered a priority in our lives and to help maintain a level of happiness and fulfillment.

CHAPTER 5

Learning from Wild Animals

"He could tell the way the animals walked that they were keeping time to some kind of music. Maybe it was the song in their own hearts that they walked to."

Laura Adams Arner, *Waterless Mountain*

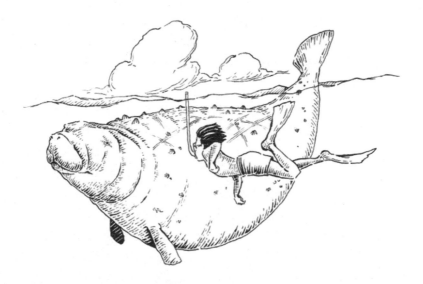

IN THE FIELD

The helicopter droned loudly as it whipped the tops of the autumn olive bushes like a hurricane. Bryce and Sierra glued their eyes to the reclaimed mine-lands of eastern Kentucky, looking for the sick cow elk. Their lips were parted in concentration, headphones clamped over their ears so they could communicate with the biologists. They scanned the open meadows for the stumbling animal.

"There it is!" Sierra announced. The bedraggled creature zigzagged as if drunk or, in reality, diseased by a tiny worm that was destroying its life. Meningeal brain worm is the most common disease among reintroduced elk, affecting the animal's central nervous system. In the late 1800s, native elk were extirpated in the wild areas of eastern United States due to overhunting. A reintroduction program has been in place to bring back the species in half a dozen states, including Kentucky.

These small parasitic worms (carried by the white-tailed deer that are resistant to the disease) travel through the body and end up in the spinal cord or brain, where they damage the nervous tissue. Infected elk become emaciated and disoriented, and waste away, starving to death. Over a four-year period, radio-collared elk in Kentucky's elk herd were monitored to determine the impact this parasitic disease had on the population. Sierra, Bryce, and I participated in this study in the summer of 2005. We were working with Dr. Karen Alexy and the Kentucky Department of Fish & Wildlife Association. Our relationship began when I traveled to the reclaimed mine lands in eastern Kentucky to write a magazine story on the state's growing elk herd and my children accompanied me to learn.

As soon as fifteen-year-old Sierra spotted the sick cow and identified it, ground control was mobilized. The wildlife technician with the rifle was informed of the elk's location, and in no time at all, the poor elk was put out of its misery, sparing the creature a slow, agonizing death. A necropsy was performed right there in the field, and Sierra and Bryce contributed right alongside their mentor, Dr. Karen Alexy.

Sierra and Bryce peeled back the hide of the elk to reveal its chest cavity. They took turns cutting the cow's ribs with loppers used for trimming branches. It sounded like celery sticks snapping as each rib was disconnected, revealing the animal's interior organs. Each vital organ was taken out and laid on the "cutting board" of the rib cage and bread-loafed into long parallel strips using a sharp knife. The lead biologist and her technicians were looking for abnormalities. The head was severed and brought back to camp, where it was sawed in half with an electric saw. There my children found the tiny stringy creature in the sheath between the brain and the skull that was causing all this trouble, the meningeal worm. This rather gruesome procedure was necessary in order to understand the disease and how it affects the elk so the Kentucky wildlife biologists can better build and manage a healthy herd. The mercy killing and resulting research was all about saving lives.

As I watched my children lean over the bloody skull of a wild animal, rubber gloves pulled on tight, working a few inches from the bone without flinching, I was rendered speechless. It made sense for Sierra to be absorbed and manage the bloody task; she was dreaming of becoming a wildlife field biologist, and this grisly procedure was giving her a chance to see what the work was like firsthand, but Bryce was right in there too. Although both children had done snake dissection at home, working on a large mammal like an elk took necropsy to a whole new level. This is what happens to children who step beyond school room walls in order to learn. They see the whole world as a classroom, even inside an elk's body on the remote Kentucky range.

This Kentucky event reminded me of my children's first memory of wild elk, which took place in a sheltered meadow high in the Montana Rockies on the Continental Divide Trail. Shortly after a high-pitched warning call pierced the air, eighty creatures suddenly thundered by in one mad surge, kicking up dust, their heavy musky smell filling the air, so close we could see the sunlight glinting in their eyes. After they passed and the dust settled, we stood there mesmerized, silent and stunned.

We had spooked them, kicked them right out of their beds, for a few hundred yards later the kids, from their perch high on their llamas, spotted dozens of flattened grass ovals. They hopped down off their llamas' backs and curled up in the beds, still warm from the elk's bodies. The kids were three and five at the time and very impressionable. This episode laid the groundwork for who they would become as adults, for wild animals taught them one of the most important lessons of their lives: empathy.

Todd and I thought that empathy was a very important virtue to teach our children because it gives you the capacity to understand or feel what another is experiencing. It enables you to put yourself in another's position, share in their emotions. Empathy strengthens our character, teaches us about kindness, respect, and dignity for all. This quality has the capacity to curb bullying and aggression, reduce prejudice and racism, and help one become more mindful of others. Empathy can be learned from encounters with human beings or through other experiences, but for Sierra and Bryce, animals taught them the most about this important virtue. Perhaps it is because animals are often helpless alongside humans, with our powers over their habitat and their lives.

I learned about empathy and animals from my father, who took me hunting as a (rebellious) teen. At home, my father and I were often at odds. He was a strict father and I was a determined kid. But when we were hunting, it was different. He taught me much about the animals but also about his love for his daughter at the same time. We would walk hand in hand in the snowy woods at the end of the day, rifles slung, more relaxed about being together than alert for an opportunity shot. To me, the kill wasn't the most important thing; connecting to the world of nature and animals and getting close to my father was. I didn't care if I shot a deer; I just loved being outdoors. Because my father took the time to take me hunting, I fell deeply in love with the natural world and have had a hard time coming indoors ever since.

I realized I would not be passing on this hunting tradition to my children when Bryce was three years old. We were out hiking when he accidentally stepped on a millipede. As he watched the guts ooze out, he broke down and began to sob. "I bet he was a nice millipede. I bet he was the *nicest* millipede and I'm the baddest boy."

I tried to explain that it was an accident and he'd never do anything like that on purpose.

"Do you think the millipede will forgive me? Do you think the millipede knows how much I loved him? Do you think the millipede will go to heaven?"

Bryce did not outgrow his intense compassion for creatures, nor did Sierra. I could not kill ants on the kitchen counter if they were present. I was instructed to scoop spiders out of the tub and deposit them outdoors. When a soggy moth was fluttering around in the toilet that had not been flushed, however, I drew the line. It warmed my heart that my children had so much compassion, but I thought, "They will never be hunters. They will probably never carry a weapon and kill a creature *on purpose.*" So I was disappointed to think that hunting would probably not be something that I would get to share with my children. But I soon realized that as advocates for nature and wildlife, we have a responsibility to pass on our knowledge and love to our children and there are certainly other ways to share and teach, besides hunting.

I began to teach them how to scout for wild animals. We went on walks to locate deer signs—the animals leave behind evidence of how they live their lives, and this fascinates all children.

We started by climbing the Blue Mountain where we live. In order to avoid some rock fields, our course was naturally funneled to a ridge. Immediately, we spotted a "lane of traffic," a faint path looking like an unmaintained hiking trail. Parallel to the trail, a little ways back, I searched for buck rubs. When I found one, I pointed out to the kids that directly underneath it, the ground was cleared to the soil by the pawing buck. Above the bare earth, in the tree, was a dead branch that the animal nibbled and licked. This resulted in killing the cambium layer that transports food to the limb, and the branch was now devoid of leaves. The buck, I explained, was leaving his scent for the does that passed by on the nearby deer trail to let them know he was here and ready to mate.

The kids excitedly hiked on ahead and found rub after rub all the way up the ridge. Many scars were healed over from previous years, indicating the trail was used continually. The bigger the buck, I told them, the earlier he rubs his scent. "So, if you find sign early in the rutting season (September), chances are a buck that sports an impressive rack made the rub."

A particular tree had a deep gouge in it, as if it were made with much aggression. "That was probably made deeper in the rut," I informed them. "It's a sign of frustration resulting from the animal's needs not being met," and the kids giggled.

As we began our descent, we found large branches that had been broken off a white oak tree that was laden with acorns. Only an animal possessing great strength such as a black bear could accomplish this. A few yards further, a chokecherry tree was annihilated. We imagined the bruin stuffing the small red berries hungrily into his mouth. It would take a lot of them to fill a big bear's stomach. The kids and I chewed on one to see what the bear's lunch tasted like and twisted our face from its pithy bitterness. Before long, we nearly stumbled into a large pile of runny dung and laughed to think of the animal making a pig of itself.

Next, we saw an old rotten log that has been rolled back and its punky fibers ripped apart and shredded. The bear was searching for grubs—little bits of food to quiet its hunger pangs.

A mud puddle by the trail revealed all sorts of tracks in the soft ground, even coyote footprints and a raccoon's tiny handprints, telling us that many kinds of animals were using the watering hole to quench their thirsts.

As we completed our descent, I talked to the kids about the glimpses we had had into the private lives of these wild animals, all neighbors that inhabit this patch of mountain in our backyard. We had observed how they spend a good part of their day—searching for food and water, watching for predators, resting, mating. All this taking place with very few humans observing them or even considering it . . . a wild world unto itself.

In becoming more aware of wild animals and their lives, we are reminded that humans are only the center of our *imagined* universe. There are billions of creatures and living species out there struggling to survive with challenges of their own, right alongside us on this planet. All are important. All have their place. I wanted my children to know this too, and what better way than to periodically immerse ourselves into *their* wild universe. If we can get them to care about the wild creatures and their home, we'll be raising stewards who will want to conduct their lives like the Native Americans who believe seven generations into the future is who we should be thinking about as we impact the planet.

MANATEES

Sierra and Bryce's deepening connection to wild animals continued over their entire childhood. When our family visited Florida and we swam with the manatees, the experience with these huge docile creatures influenced Sierra into pursuing a career in wildlife biology.

Because of the natural warm springs found on the gulf side of Florida, many manatees winter over there, particularly in the Crystal River Wildlife Refuge. These springs emit billions of gallons of seventy-two-degree water per day out of caverns in the earth. The Florida Fish and Wildlife Conservation Commission created this unique refuge back in 1983, the only one of its kind, specifically for the protection of the endangered Florida manatee. There are forty acres of winter sanctuary including a roped-off area behind buoys where the animals can retreat when they want to avoid boats, divers, and snorkelers.

The sheer size of the creatures (some weighing up to 3,000 pounds) made us feel quite small, for their bulk blocked everything when they approached us. But we found the silence of their underwater world startling and peaceful. The manatees rolled over gracefully and presented their bellies for us to stroke. The kids reached out their little hands and petted their leathery bodies. One came up and nuzzled Sierra's mask, its soft face and long whiskers brushing her.

Sierra hung in the water, her wetsuit making her buoyant, and stared at the manatees' huge bodies. They were blimp-like, as though blown up with air, with barnacles on their backs and long white scars where they had been hit by boat propellers. She examined their mangled tails. Some had big chunks ripped away. There were so many injured that the Florida Fish & Game had over nine hundred manatees on record, identified by their scars.

Sierra was visibly moved, her eyes growing wide and watery under her mask, as she pointed to the worst victims. She felt very sad to see what had happened to these beautiful creatures that aren't able to defend themselves from predators, much less boats. Here in the refuge, they swam up to us out of curiosity and the fact that they chose to be with us, to seek human interaction, felt extraordinary. Sierra told me that swimming with the manatees reminded her of the Native American saying "Mitakuye Oyasin" ("All My Relations"), a Lakota phrase of oneness and harmony with all life forms, which reflects their worldview of interconnectedness.

A teenage Sierra wrote in her journal:

My heart was first ignited on our family's travels. It was the magical moments on the Continental Divide Trail where I squatted on a beaver dam in bare feet watching a furry face tug a leafy bough across the water, or feeling the ground shake as a stampede of elk thundered across the trail with galloping bulls and spindly-legged calves bellowing and snorting.

When I was eleven, I paddled through remote Thai lagoons, the treetops bouncing with gibbons. I worked with wolves at an institute in Minnesota, kayaked with hundreds of grey seals in Kouchibouquac NP in New Brunswick, and boated amongst flocks of exotic, pink flamingos on the Yucatan Peninsula. I also canoed through Georgia's Okefenokee Swamp spotting sixty alligators a day, and snorkeled with Loggerhead sea turtles in Mexico.

These one-on-one experiences with wild animals in their natural surroundings, doing the sports that I love, took a strong hold in my young heart. I wanted to study and protect them so they would be here for future generations to fall in love with like I did.

Throughout our kids' childhood, Todd and I continually sought out memorable ways to interact with wild animals while incorporating travel and outdoor adventures at the same time. We were encouraged to do so partly because of Sierra's growing interest in pursuing a future occupation as a wildlife biologist, but I knew that regardless of her career choices, the impact, magic, and beauty of these experiences were reason enough to show up.

Over a period of a few years, Sierra made a deep connection with Dr. Karen Alexy while working in Kentucky's elk range. She communicated with Karen on a regular basis, asking advice on projects, direction, and choices she was considering in regards to her future. Although both children were involved in their ongoing work in Kentucky and both benefited from the knowledge and experience, this work spoke especially deeply to Sierra's soul.

Both kids were invited back to work in the field again and again and again, often without me. I would drop them off in the Kentucky mine lands and go off to do research for other stories. On those annual trips, Karen took Sierra and Bryce on bear and coyote trapping excursions, taught them how to track using radio telepathy and night vision goggles. They learned to tattoo bear lips as a means of future identification, and to insert a gloved hand up a sedated elk's anus and pull out pellets to see if it was shedding any worms. They studied organisms under a microscope and drove a four-wheeler in the mine lands. Over the course of these days, my children came to understand what goes into managing a herd of wild animals.

Both children returned to Kentucky the next spring to help "catch calves." They searched the thickets for small, spotted, newly born calves, slid radio collars over their necks, collected measurements, drew blood, stapled in ear tags, and took their weights. The herd has expanded to ten thousand strong and is now thriving despite setbacks from diseases like meningeal worm.

Sierra and Bryce laughed and teased Karen and the techs as they played cards in the evenings and cooked community meals. They all lived together in the clubhouse, and overcame their age and education gaps quite effortlessly. Besides the knowledge base my children were forming, their ability to live and work alongside professional adults, who not only accepted them but embraced their company and their assistance, taught them volumes and built their confidence tremendously.

Dr. Karen Alexy was special to go out of her way to do this for my children. Some professionals would not give teenagers the time of day until they became a graduate student who could professionally benefit them. Parents may face a challenge in finding open and generous human beings who would invite young students into their world, but it is not impossible, especially when they see that their child's interest is passionate.

After Sierra's very positive experiences with Dr. Karen Alexy in the Kentucky mine lands, she continued her exploration by seeking opportunities with local wildlife biologists. She was old enough, at seventeen, to make her own connections and her time in Kentucky gave her the confidence to believe her involvement in their research would be an asset. Sierra targeted nearby Hawk Mountain Sanctuary, which, in addition to being a wild bird sanctuary, is an international center for raptor conservation, education, observation, and research.

The biologists there, as well as other biologists in the county, took her under their wings, as they tramped the woods together doing field work. She participated in small mammal studies, bird counts, raptor trapping, and deer and bear aging. She learned how to rub her finger over bear molars and test for wear, measure deer antlers and gauge growth as well as check hooves for maggots and general health problems. She caught ovenbirds and chickadees in mist nets, learned to measure wingspan and weigh and insert tiny bands on their feet to track them. She installed nesting tubes, monitored mating and learned that by studying the animals' habits and population, we can glean infinite amounts of knowledge on the planet's health and how it relates to us. These opportunities provided Sierra with the chance to rub shoulders with experts, stretch beyond her age group and provided her with valuable information on choosing a career path.

All the life experiences a parent exposes their children to during their formative years influence and impact who they decide to become and what they will choose to value. At the same time, two siblings can share in the same experience, yet something can click and resonate with one far more than the other, so that they go on to create a life out of it. As parents, we must have our antennas up. We must vigilantly watch for clues as to how we can best direct them and cultivate their interests.

"SAVING LIVES" BY SEVENTEEN-YEAR-OLD SIERRA

The following essay, written by Sierra when she was a teenager, beautifully illustrates the impact wild creatures can have on a young adult, shaping her into who she will ultimately become and guiding her toward the life work she will choose to do.

This past May a Great Blue Heron dropped out of the sky and into our garden. I was about to open the garden gate to cut the asparagus when I saw the bird. Why had it not taken flight in fear? It did not move more than its saffron eye, which it bolted to my stare. This was not natural. I abandoned the asparagus and strode swiftly back to the house to tell my family. We went about our business the rest of the morning, hoping nature would call it back to the river.

But the heron was still there by afternoon, and had moved little more than two feet. It looked tired and weeping, like it had abandoned its fate to stand in our garden until it fell over in weakness.

My mom called the local wildlife rehab center and they told us to bring it in. To catch it, we had to dress in armor, to protect ourselves from its slender bill wielded like a dagger in self-defense, targeting our eyeballs. Herons are merciless creatures when they are protecting themselves. They strike at the eyes to blind their enemies, or their saviors. Birds don't judge. So, my brother and I pulled on hoodies and tightened the strings around our faces, knotting them so we could only peer through a tiny hole. On our eyes, we wore safety and swimming goggles.

However, the poor bird was so disoriented, my dad merely walked up to it as we came in from the sides and tipped a five-gallon bucket over its stocky frame. It hardly resisted. My mom and I drove it to the wildlife center, with a board bungeed to the top of the bucket.

When the wildlife rehabilitator opened the lid she swiftly grabbed it by the bill and curled its stick-like frame into her armpit. Apparently, despite its size, the heron only weighed one pound. It is a hollow bird. She was convinced it had been poisoned, probably flew into a cloud of pesticides that was sprayed on the nearby Christmas tree farms. She gave it an antidote injection and figured she could revive it within a couple of weeks.

We shut the trunk, slipped her a twenty-dollar bill for the medicine. She said she would call us in a week and let us know how the heron was doing. Driving away, we knew we had done all that we could.

That night I thought about the heron. Even adults find it hard to accept the possibility that animals, that people, will die despite our efforts to save them. As children, we work even harder to save them. We hope even harder. We believe that we can make a difference if we try.

When my brother Bryce and I were growing up, whenever our cats killed a creature, we would bury it in "Forest Park." Forest Park was a little patch of woods where we dug a small "pond" into forest loam, lined with a piece of plastic. We dug a grave for every animal that died and wrapped the poor bedraggled creature in a blanket of leaves. Then we said a prayer and covered the leaves with dirt. We used old bricks as headstones and scratched their names with a blunt stone. We would wander through the orchard and llama pasture gathering a small fistful of flowers to lay on the fresh grave.

Sometimes the animals were not fully dead when my brother and I rescued them, traumatized, hearts pounding from our cats' jowls. Cupping them in our hands, tears streaming down our cheeks, one of us would cradle the bird or vole while the other locked the cats in the sunroom and got a cardboard box from storage. We would fill the box with cotton balls and leaves and fill a bottle cap from the recycling bin with water. Out in the chicken shed, we would steal a small handful of grain or corn and sprinkle it in the box. Sometimes we did more *extensive research into the animal's diet using field guides to North American mammals to find a list of foodstuff the particular animal sustained itself on.*

It didn't cross our minds that the animal was in its death throes and probably not concerned with matters of food. But we had hope and we would try everything we could. Bryce and I would make up songs to sing to them. Usually they were dead by morning and we quietly got the shovel and headed reverently to Forest Park for the burial.

The graveyard became quite extensive over the years. Our cats had free reign of the great outdoors and they deposited the crumpled bodies on the doormat as presents. Anytime one of us opened the sunroom door and stepped onto the mat with a soft crunch of a rodent beneath our feet, we would scurry for the shovel and head to Forest Park. This became our ritual.

Soon there were several dozen bricks forming a semicircle around the puddle in Forest Park. There were birds, chipmunks, voles, mice, frogs, moles, and baby bunnies buried there. My brother and I tended the graves as well. Periodically we would clear the falling leaves and forest debris out of respect for the animals, re-etch the names onto the bricks with a stone from the driveway, and pick fresh wild flowers.

My brother and I rescued tadpoles too, when the rains came and the pond beside the back porch flooded. The pond was only ten feet across, not much more than a puddle. We watched the frogs come in the spring, the first sign winter was ending. One would appear floating on the dark surface stained with tannic acid from the rotting leaves. Sometimes there was ice still floating in the pond when the frogs came. We would run and tell my mom and we would all stand at the edge of the pond and celebrate the arrival of spring.

Over the next week more and more frogs would appear, croaking hoarsely and filling the woods with song. Bryce and I would creep onto the back porch, and sneak over to the railing, peering between the wooden bars to watch their masses—sometimes fifty or sixty frogs in this tiny puddle. Their song would cease the moment one of us would laugh and betray our presence. Then slowly they would take up song again and begin their copulating.

This was how my brother and I learned about how babies are made: watching frog sex. The female frogs were a buff tan, the color of buckskin. They were easy to see flailing and kicking limbs as six or eight male frogs competed to attach themselves to her. Sometimes Bryce and I wanted to save her, to net her out of the roiling mass of males. But my mom would gently stop us and tell us to put the net away. We needed to let the frogs alone when they were mating. I was often surprised the female frog survived the affair.

But in a couple days we would find the mass of green jelly lulling in the sun-warmed shallows of the pond. This was another cause to celebrate as we cupped a clump of the shivering jelly, black specks like tiny pupils that would slowly develop and unfurl into tadpoles. The jelly acting as a magnifying lens for my brother and me to watch their evolution. Soon, a tail would sprout and a tiny head would take form. Then one day the sheaths of jelly would split open and tiny flicking tadpoles would lie in the skin of water on top of the eggs. This was when life became dangerous for the tadpoles and Bryce and I took over their protection.

When the summer thunderstorms came and the pond overflowed, the tadpoles went too. Bryce and I would crouch in our underwear, armed with white plastic spoons. We worked as fast as we could, scooping squirming tadpoles into plastic cups which we poured back into the pond. We had to build a dam to back the water, hoping the rocks would act as a screen to hold the tadpoles back.

I remember one rain where the tadpoles were washed all the way through the woods and down the driveway. People say that children have short attention spans, but my brother and I slaved for hours squatting in the pouring rain, our shirts clinging to our backs, our hair hanging in strings. We only gave up when the sun went down and we could no longer see the squirming black beads. I remember feeling devastated as we abandoned the rest to dry up and die.

And now at seventeen years old I still feel strongly about saving wild animals, be it tadpoles or a sick Great Blue Heron. A week later we got a call from the wildlife rehabilitator. The heron was dead. The amount of poison the bird ingested was much more than she thought, enough to be lethal. She stayed up all night with the bird as it shook and lurched, squawking and contracting its yellow claws until it died an excruciatingly painful death. Peggy said it was the worst case she had ever dealt with. She too was crying all night as the heron died.

We all mourned the heron. Its death felt like a tragedy. Maybe this was because we had invested time and energy into saving it. Whether it lived or died meant something to us. Perhaps others would have looked at the shaking heron standing in their garden and seeing that it was clearly on the brink of death, would have turned away and let nature take its course, like tadpoles washed from flooding ponds, and predatory cats hunting prey. Cats have to eat. Only so many tadpoles can grow into frogs. But at the same time is it wrong to have empathy for a creature facing death? Even if it is inevitable that the tadpoles will only be washed out from the pond in the next storm that the mangled mouse will die of internal bleeding in the night, doesn't it mean something that at least we tried to save them?

Perhaps that's why it meant so much to me to try to save the heron. Its death wasn't something that happens in nature. It wasn't right that pesticides, applied by humans, had poisoned the heron. I felt responsible for the deeds of my species. I had to try to revive it, to save its life.

I will admit that I do not run to the pond with plastic spoons when the rains come anymore. When I find a dead rodent on the stoop I no longer dig a grave and pick flowers. But I do usually whisper a prayer when I carry it to the edge of the yard and fling its body into the woods. I still care. Those days as a child saving tadpoles have stayed with me.

NUTS AND BOLTS

Many professionals are happy to take on a helper or an intern if they are made aware that a student is passionate and interested. It never hurts to ask and as parents, we need to believe that what our children need as far as an education, they deserve. Make sure you discuss how your child can help them with their work, that it is possible for the mentorship to be a two-way street. Learn to network yourself, and then teach your child to network, because as they grow older, a request has more impact coming from the student themselves. Volunteering in studies, counts, or field work projects as a family gives your child confidence to later go on and work on their own. Once they are older, job shadowing is a very useful resource for young people to get a taste for an occupation or an activity. Internships and apprenticeships are the next step as your child grows into adulthood.

CHAPTER 6

Learning from Other Faith Cultures

"One sees clearly only with the heart. Anything essential is invisible to the eye."

Antoine de Saint-Exuprey, *The Little Prince*

"A DAY IN MARRAKECH"
BY FIFTEEN-YEAR-OLD BRYCE

The following essay, written by Bryce when he was a teenager, shows his sharp eye, his attention to detail, and his great love of variety, which has served him well in his career as an artist.

The time is 5 a.m. The city of Marrakech, Morocco, is breathlessly quiet. Suddenly, chanting begins to resound from a nearby mosque. Within moments it is followed by a chorus of guttural voices, emanating from over one hundred minarets. Asleep on a rooftop terrace I am jarred awake by the thunderous Call to Prayer. This is our Moroccan alarm clock.

From our rooftop terrace we have a sprawling view of the city. The markets form a web of convoluted streets; alleyways thatched in bamboo and hopelessly tangled. From the central plaza, the streets radiate outward in a labyrinth capable of making anyone feel directionally challenged. In the distance loom the snow-capped Atlas Mountains.

Departing from our rooftop we gravitate towards the plaza. By the time the sun had ascended, monkey-handlers and snake charmers are already welcoming the day. People are everywhere, mummified women in shawls, filthy children, wizened old folks with canes, teenagers swerving erratically on mopeds, and beggars shielded under cardboard, aligning cigarette butts with Mecca.

After breakfast in the plaza we take the plunge into the markets. Everything is rich in color-vibrant scarves, jewelry, teapots, and tasseled rugs. Tables are heaped with camel-leather saddles, daggers, spices, and fresh produce. Our personal favorites are the stands piled with figs and dates. In the center of the stands are holes where Moroccans pop up to collect our order, reminiscent of prairie dogs emerging from their burrows.

"One moment please!" they shout. "Just look, no buy! Like free!"

Animals are also numerous. Donkeys haul carts containing every product from Coca-Cola bottles to propane tanks. Cats wander the streets, scavenging bits of meat and gnawing at fish bones. Roosters peck at the ground.

We wander between cracked, sunset-colored walls until we detect the stench of the tannery. The tannery is an open area with vats of water made milky with pigeon droppings. Workers slosh in the rank broth in nothing but shorts, laboring to tan sheep leather. It looks like a *vast honeycomb, where men hang skins to dry and mangy cats wander the rims. We are handed sprigs of mint leaf to sniff to dull the stench.*

At the dyers' souk, pieces of cloth are hung from lines and lifted with hooked poles. The colors are striking and vary from crimson to turquoise and cobalt blue. We climb up a spiral staircase to view the scenery from the terrace. Somehow, we find ourselves bargaining with a man who offers eight thousand camels in exchange for my sister.

By nightfall the plaza is a hive of humanity. Like moths to a flame, we are attracted towards its lit center. Men wheel in food carts and cooking tents, banishing the snake charmers and their repetitive song. Soon pungent smoke clouds the air. Small greasy chefs busily fry small greasy sausages. Buckets of snails entice the passersby. Determined tattoo artists pursue us with syringes of henna, while we pursue the aroma of frying food.

The traffic is chaotic, mopeds swerving around bewildered tourists. The whine of motorbikes pierces the air.

"Where you from?" inquires a fruit salesman.

"The United States."

"A thousand welcomes," he exclaims, grinning gleefully. We smile back.

From dawn to dusk the markets have ensnared us. We realize a week would not be fully sufficient to see all the wonders of Marrakech. Returning to our rooftop terrace, we hear the fifth and final Call to Prayer, while below us drummers pound out the heartbeat of Marrakech.

All this occurred in just twenty-four hours. When we traveled to a foreign country such as Morocco, where nearly everything was strange, exotic, and new, what occurred in the mornings always felt it had happened many days ago. Time felt stretched and packed with abundant experiences. This is one of the treasures of travel, a lengthening of days, of your life. My husband often felt like he should be staying home to work but I told him, when you lay dying, your memories sweetening your last days will not be those about work but of the days spent wandering the souk of Morocco. Sierra and Bryce learned this early in life.

Our family traveled to Morocco in 2008 to celebrate the kids' sixteenth and eighteenth birthdays. Our friend, Allen Hoppes, owner of "I, Like You, Tours," was broadening his guide service to include private trips for families. He needed a family to practice on and we happily obliged. Allen believed, as we do, that travel can be much more than moving from one place to another.

When my sister learned that we were splurging on this month-long adventure, she replied, "If that were me, I would be using that money for my children's education."

To that I replied, "I am."

It had been eight years since the attack on the Twin Towers when we traveled to Morocco and fear had been driven into many American hearts, including an imperceptive fear of Muslims in general. Todd and I wanted to teach our children acceptance and respect for all people. The best way to have that happen was to go to a Muslim country and live there for a time.

Another of our goals was seeking a deeper understanding of a people and their lives. Cross-cultural travel makes you aware and sensitive of another's feelings, resulting in more tolerance and acceptance. When this occurs, we can more easily reach a place of cooperation between people, communities, and nations. Todd and I felt this trait was necessary in order for our children and future generations to work successfully across cultures. It promotes a global mindset.

It may take a little more courage to travel with your family to a country like Morocco, where we may be called upon to leave our comfort zone. Not everything is delightful, but it is real. We make sure to select destinations where, if we do leave our comfort zone, we do not leave our safety zone, and guides like Allen Hoppes helped.

One of the best ways of getting to know a country is by walking the streets with local people. In the cities of Morocco, we observed that Muslim women rarely go out in public. "The street is a man's domain,"

Allen told us. When women do go out, they huddle in twos and walk tightly arm in arm as if one being.

Their children play away from the streets, protected. The women go up to the rooftops to hang their wash, feel the sun, and see the view. Even if it was only a scene of more rooftops, this is where they socialize and share with their friends. The women feel "safe" on the roof from the rest of the world—the world of men—as they do inside their homes. (Over half of Moroccan women have little education and cannot read or write.)

The other place to socialize is the hammam, the public bath. Here they scrub one another in long, rough strokes up and down their backs until the dead skin came off in black spaghetti strings. How different from our culture where women not only bathe alone, they often lock the bathroom door to ensure privacy.

As we walked the streets, dark-haired, handsome young Moroccan men, dressed in all black, were everywhere, with seemingly nothing to do with their time.

Sierra wrote about them in her journal, *"They all make eye contact with me and latch on with a desirous look. They lock their dark eyes shamelessly on mine and coo, 'oh, la la.' I look away bashfully. One stops dead in his tracks and just stares at me. And I was on Mom's arm wearing a coat and a hat and not having showered in days, I wasn't feeling attractive. Bryce tries to get me to walk fifty feet ahead of the rest of the group to see the level of harassment that is inflicted on me. I got quite a few marriage offers from shop owners and one jokingly offers nine hundred thousand camels to be his wife. Allen later told us that this is a very old Moroccan joke—offering animals to pretty tourists in exchange for their hand."*

In Morocco, Sierra was different and so she got noticed. She had no competition with other young Moroccan women, since they were not on the streets, and we saw no American tourists, especially young adults. Remaining hidden in your home and behind scarves when you do go out in public began to make more sense to my daughter.

Aspects of life in Morocco were not only different for us, they were at times both amusing and a bit challenging. But isn't that the point of all travel—to arrive at a point of deeper understanding? We learned to navigate the streets of Morocco, not just through the maze of the souk, but also amongst their people.

The Moroccan women in the rural areas, we discovered, have more freedom than their urban sisters but also more work. They must go out daily to collect greens for cow food and lug huge bundles of sticks on their backs from the forest to fuel their cook fires. The rural men leaned against telephone poles or alongside buildings. They looked hard at us for not many tourists visited the places Allen took us. This uneven division of labor was noted by my children.

Our most impactful experiences in Morocco, the ones that taught us the most, were the times spent in the private homes of the rural people, where we could see who they really were. Towards the end of our month-long stay, Allen arranged a homestay experience where we walked from one family's rural farm to their relatives'.

Firstborn males are often named Mohamed and in this particular blended family of two second marriages, there were two sons named Mohamed as well as their father. Three Mohameds under the same roof! Back in America, many teens put tremendous energy into finding out "who they are" and creating a separate identity from their parents so my kids found this very unique.

We ate with the family around one massive bowl of community food, consuming what was right in front of us, with one hand (the right hand, because your left is considered "unclean"). My kids feared they were straying too far to the left or right and stuck to mopping up meat juice with hunks of bread to play it safe. It's difficult to overeat and get fat in this country if you just eat the food that's immediately in front of you.

Afterwards, the Moroccan family asked us questions, with the aid of Allen interpreting.

"I've heard that in some countries like America you eat from your own plate, but I have never seen this."

When our hosts learned that I am five years older than Todd, they replied that in Morocco, a woman is never allowed to marry a younger man. A woman must go to live with her husband's family, and her new mother-in-law becomes her constant companion. The married couples do not sleep together; the men and boys sleep in a separate room.

My children sat there quietly, absorbing this information and processing it in relation to our family. After a while, our host asked if Sierra and I would like to dress up in their traditional style of clothing. Colorful striped wool blankets were wrapped tightly around our waists, black kohl eye liner was applied to our eyes, and a head scarf wound tight around our heads, tucking in our hair "to protect us," they said.

Our host and hostess's combined marriage gave them six children, ranging from a toddler to kids in their late teens. Sierra and Bryce bonded with them very quickly. The young Moroccan boys hung on my kids affectionately with their arms draped around their shoulders. They tried on Bryce's aviator sunglasses trying to look "gangster" for photos. They got my kids to teach them American lyrics and they sang together, giggling. They wanted to play simple card games as a way to overcome the language barrier.

Bryce wrote in his journal: *"After learning that they loved hip hop music, we sang Akon songs, cracking up laughing at their strong accents. Here were these kids, who rode donkeys bareback in the remote Moroccan hills, but shared with us the same love of music. The jokes we told, the card games we played, made us connect despite our drastically different upbringings. We were just kids, going through life in separate corners of the world, yet our youthful spirit felt the same."*

At the end of the evening, when they directed our family to split up for the night as was their custom, Allen informed them that our family would remain together. Although we were sleeping on narrow sofas that lined the walls, not in double beds, our hosts still made a point to direct Sierra and me to the far opposite side of the room from my husband and her brother. They tried to get Allen to sleep with the other men, but he too said that he would be staying with "the family."

When we said good-bye the next morning, there were warm hugs all around and many photos taken to preserve the memory. The Islamic people have a beautiful saying, "Guests are gifts from God," and this Moroccan family represented this sentiment beautifully! We hoped to see one another again and to that they replied with the equally beautiful Arabic phrase, "inshallah," God willing, or if Allah wills.

My children claimed that out of the dozen countries they experienced before they went to college, Morocco was at the top of the list. The people were extraordinarily welcoming hosts, a monumental lesson to learn about accepting and understanding other cultures and religions. Through it, Sierra and Bryce learned to look for similarities, understand differences, and not be fooled by inaccurate perceptions.

After our trip, Allen shared these thoughts of our experience with my children:

"Many cultural norms (what we eat, when we eat, whom we marry, which God we worship, how we dress, what is important to us) carry the weight of habit, history and peer pressure. When we travel, we begin to see that other people do things differently, think differently. They may also think their ways are the best, right, natural and true ways of doing things or being. They might even think their ways are sacred and come directly from God. With enough travel and enough exposure, an intelligent mind recognizes that there are many different versions of "normal." We learn that we don't have to eat only what is put on the plate in front of us. We don't have to listen to Fox or CNN to find out what dog tastes like or what Muslims think—we can go find out personally. We can educate ourselves and decide what works best for us."

Our children learned from Allen and their experience in Morocco that fear often comes from not understanding something, from the unknown. When we travel and experience things for ourselves, we are less likely to be scared of those who are different from us. In the end, traveling and learning can create more understanding in the world and thus, perhaps more peace. Isn't this one of the most important gifts of learning we can give our children?

When we traveled to countries that were off the normal tourists' radars—independently and not connected to a tour group—we definitely got noticed. We couldn't help but stick out. We looked like Americans. Our behavior was being noted and then compared to what they might hear in the news or on television.

On a trip abroad, I was once approached by a foreigner from a developing country who was puzzled that we felt comfortable leaving our homes or were able to go out of our homes. "You might live in mansions," he said, "but the street is a very dangerous place." When I asked him what he based his information on, he admitted it was two American TV shows, *Lifestyles of the Rich and Famous* and *NYPD Blue*. He thought that was how we *all* lived.

The travel writer Pico Iyer wrote, "In traveling, we become a kind of carrier pigeon—in transporting back and forth what every culture needs. We carry values and beliefs and news to the places we go, and in many parts of the world, we become walking video screens and living newspapers, the only channels that can take people out of the censored limits of their homeland."

We met people from Switzerland while in Morocco, and they said, "What a shame that all Americans are viewed in relation to your country's politics, the behavior of (then) President Bush, and judge you accordingly." Another asked, "Why do you Americans think that you're better than everyone else?"

To that I replied, "I don't, and I am not my country's politics nor my country's government nor my country's leader."

It was very beneficial for Sierra and Bryce to see how other people in the world viewed us. Conversely, these encounters provided opportunities to take the common misperceptions of foreigners and turn them into more accurate and real portrayals about who Americans are. At the same time, this process helped us confront our own ignorance when it came to other cultures.

Americans have a reputation in the world for being quite ignorant about the world and perhaps a bit naïve in believing that the things the United States government does in our name are all to help foreign people and countries. Americans like to think that everyone in the world wants to live in America, or be like Americans, when the reality is something else. Traveling did not destroy our American ideas, but it simply gave us a reality check.

After our trip to Morocco, the Call to Prayer—broadcasting from the minarets, piercing the skyline, echoing through the narrow winding streets and bouncing off the rooftops—was forever a call to us too, no matter our religious affiliation or which name we called our spirit guide. For us, it was a call to stop for a moment and reflect on our life, all that we had and the opportunity to make a difference right there in that time that we had found ourselves in. Five times a day we are reminded to be grateful and that we are blessed.

One of the great gifts of traveling to Morocco, a majority-Muslim country, was our piqued interest in world religions. The Unitarian Universalist (UU) Church, where Sierra and Bryce were raised, spoke loud and clear to them: their message is one of acceptance and broad thinking. We connected to the way wisdom was gleaned from all the world religions, drawing from scripture and science, nature and philosophy, personal experience and ancient tradition.

After we returned from Morocco, Sierra immersed herself in a project she entitled "What do you Believe?" where she sent a survey to fifty family friends and asked them a few dozen questions about their beliefs. It sparked an interest in local religions and we set out to experience as many as possible.

Our UU religious instructors put Sierra and Bryce in touch with local Buddhists and they attended a Zen Buddhist Meditation and Worship. After hearing a detailed explanation about the whys and hows of their practices, they learned to chant and do sitting and walking meditations.

Jewish friends made us their special guests at their Seder—a Jewish ritual feast that marks the beginning of the Jewish holiday of Passover. We listened to the story of the Exodus from three thousand years ago, our friends reading from a Haggadah. We participated by speaking responses, singing songs, sampling the Seder plate of food, toasting with goblets of wine, and eating delicious kosher food.

Our UU Church arranged a day-long Native American Retreat for the religious youth group where they did ceremonies involving the Four Directions, participated in a sweat lodge, created personal prayer banners, and danced a "Long Dance" in order to reach a meditative state.

The Old Order Mennonite Service in the farmlands of Kutztown, PA, Berks County, however, was perhaps their most fascinating religious experience.

From Sierra's journal:

The morning began with images: a line of horse drawn buggies, bikes leaning against trees, boys dressed in pressed dark trousers and sky-blue shirts; girls wearing subdued dresses and bonnets. All were barefoot with dirt-stained toes. Inside the plain church, women sat separately from the men. Wooden floors, wooden pews, white walls, no cross or symbol to indicate it was a holy place.

Despite their "Sunday best," it was interesting how beefy the women's arms looked, their fingers gnarled and their nails rimmed in dirt. It looked like they had been out that morning digging onions. I really felt self-conscious and half-naked even wearing the most conservative clothes I own.

The ministers sat in the center with their backs to us. Their small table is called "The Singing Table," where the elder men sit and pray, sing the High German songs, and lead the congregation through the chorus.

The words, nasally and rumbling deep from the throat, floated on the breeze through the open windows. I felt like I had time warped as I gazed around at the black-rimmed caps hanging in rows against the white-washed walls. The church was filled with the sound of whimpering babies, shuffling feet, and whinnying horses from the buggies outside.

The three ministers read from the hymnal book printed in 1800 and made an improvised service of whatever comes to them. The woman next to us said that while the elders do that, the congregation sits here praying that they will have something to say. She volunteered to translate the entire service onto a notepad. When we flipped through her notes, it contained the basic "resist temptation, do not lie, do not steal" messages.

The congregation did not appear to be too evoked in passion. The older folks' heads drooped into their laps, others tilted their heads back in sleep, the young boys played with a string on the curtain behind them or chased flies around the room with their eyes. Pig-tailed girls squirmed in their mother's laps and flipped through little books about life on a farm with pictures of little kids that looked just like them, dressed in bonnets and suspenders.

It was an incredible experience that truly was like traveling back in time. It stunned me how this old-fashioned community so deeply and strictly immersed in its heritage manages to exist parallel to our insanely technological and modern society.

Sierra drew the conclusion that everyone's search for truth and meaning was quite similar to everyone else's regardless of what name they gave their god. Trying to discover our reason for existence, our purpose, while attempting to be the best people we can be, was universal. In the end, that was all that mattered.

TURKEY

Seven years after our trip to Morocco, Bryce and I returned to a Muslim country, this time to Turkey. Bryce created a travel guide to Istanbul for his illustration class at the Tyler School of Art at Temple University. I thought Turkey would be a fitting destination for a graduation trip. We could visit the attractions he spent a semester researching and then painting.

I purchased our flights far in advance (eleven months), and soon after, ISIS began to wreak havoc in the Middle East. The Syrian-Turkish border had become a dangerous hot spot. Our friends and family questioned the wisdom of this destination. I sought the advice of my nephew, who worked for the Department of State, and he told me that as long as we avoided the border, and diligently watched the news, he certainly advised going. In fact, he bought a ticket himself and joined us. We never felt afraid or at risk; the Turkish people were nothing but extremely welcoming. The two places that we traveled, Istanbul and Cappadocia in the central part of the country, were—even at that time—being visited by many tourists.

It was in a bus shelter in the Cappadocian region of central Turkey that we were once again reminded of how often our misperceptions come into play and how we can reach out and connect in spite of them.

The old woman's scarf wrapped around her neck and head covered all visible signs of hair, what color it was or how little was left. I couldn't be accurate in judging her age. On her robust body, she wore a long, gathered skirt, a blouse, and a knitted button-down vest. On her large feet were old sneakers. Holding a cloth bag by its handles, she sat on the bench waiting for a bus to take her to the nearby town of Avenos. She watched me, smiling. She was trying to figure us out.

Speaking in broken English with a thick Turkish accent, she attempted to start a conversation by asking, "Are you from America?"

"Yes."

"Is that your husband?"

"No, it's my son."

"More children?"

"A daughter."

"Is *that* your daughter?" (She was referring to a Korean girl standing next to me whom I exchanged small talk with.)

"No!" We all laughed. She blushed and laughed too.

When the bus pulled up, the old woman got in first. Bryce and I carefully picked our way down the narrow aisle trying not to bump into anyone. All the seats were filled. When I passed my new friend, who had scored a seat, she patted her knee and offered her lap for me to sit on. I was touched.

I thought about our friends back home who were fearful of Turkey. If they could see my old friend now, they too might feel silly. We

Americans have to leave our homes and travel to foreign places to see for ourselves so that we can accurately learn who these people truly are—and have them understand who we are. Had it not been a short bus ride, I may have taken her up on her offer.

NUTS AND BOLTS

To help better prepare a family for this sort of travel, the US Department of State has a service called "Learn About Your Destination," where they provide specific information on every country of the world. They discuss topics like when tropical storm season is, where to be cautious of crime, visa requirements, the latest political relations between the United States and the selected country, areas of unrest to avoid, what vaccinations are recommended, how many passport pages are required for the visa, road conditions during rainy season, etc.

The US State Department issues two types of travel advisories: alerts and warnings. An alert means travelers should take precautions, that there exists a somewhat heightened, though temporary risk. For this type of alert, the department does not recommend canceling plans. You can notify the embassy of your travel plans if an alert has been issued. The program is called STEP (Smart Traveler Enrollment Program). It makes it easier to receive security messages and to be located by the US government in the event of an emergency. In country, elections may spur protests or unrest and it is good to be aware of news and events like these. Sometimes just avoiding crowds and staying alert makes good sense. The challenge of getting economical flights far enough out to ensure a discounted fare leaves you susceptible to last minute political troubles. Most travel insurance does not cover cancellation because of civil unrest. Purchasing CFAR (cancel for any reason coverage) insurance may be considered if you are traveling to a part of the world that is prone to unrest. It costs a little more but may be worth it. It's also important to read the warnings very carefully because security levels vary from region to region.

To feel more comfortable in a country where customs are very different from your own or where there is a large risk of being misunderstood, perhaps a personal guide for your family would take some stress away. It would depend on where you were going and what you were doing. When Bryce and I went to Turkey, we went to two tourist destinations and there was much material available to help us plan our own private trip. On the other hand, when our family toured all over the country of Morocco, we wanted to immerse the kids in more cultural experiences and off-the-beaten path destinations, so we opted for a personal guide to take us there and show them to us. A decision can depend on your mode of transportation too. Driving a rental car can be a nightmare in a country like Morocco where road signs are written in characters with no possible way of reading them.

CHAPTER 7

Learning from Independent Travel

"A prudent person avoids unpleasant things; but a wise man overcomes them."

Michael Lipman, *The Chatterlings*

PLANES, TRAINS, AND BUSES

PLANES IN RUSSIA

Navigating transportation can be one of your greatest challenges when traveling independently in a foreign country. You will encounter situations where absolutely nothing on your part can be done; the outcome will be beyond your control. In those instances, what a tour guide would normally handle, you must handle on your own. You must also resist the tendency to feel like you are being victimized and learn to be flexible.

From our view inside the locked and secluded lounge at the Moscow Airport, it looked like the dead of night outside. It was nine in the morning. The entire runway was shrouded in an icy mist, as if the very air were frosted like glass. The parked airplanes looked like the frozen remnants of a past civilization, recovered from glacial ice. By 10 a.m., conditions hadn't improved much. Our family was hiding here for two days and nights, sentenced to this prison of sorts by the airport authorities. We had no blanket or pillow for sleeping, only peanuts and water for sustenance, and we were told we could not leave. We felt like Tom Hanks in the film *Terminal*.

We slumped on rigid chairs and looked out at the frozen wasteland. We were not surprised that everyone we encountered through this unexpected fiasco appeared to be miserable. America had just put sanctions on Russia, so the United States was not looked upon fondly by many Russians. Maybe the freezing environment had something to do with their seemingly hopeless and depressing attitude. We had to fight the tendency to join in.

Half a year ago, I purchased flights to China via Russia for my family. I did not think that we would arrive in Moscow to discover that our next leg to Bangkok was canceled and planes would not be flying for two more days. A Russian airline had offered the roundtrip tickets at a considerable savings compared to other airlines. When the clerk informed us that we could not go out of the airport to get a hotel as we had no visa, we were shocked and helpless. Visas had to be applied for ahead of time. We could not stay at the airport that long either, she informed us, because that was against the airport rules. We had no idea what to do. They had no idea what to do. We went to the American consulate's office at the airport and they could do nothing. Authorities then ushered us into the empty lounge where we sat waiting. On the second day, I demanded that I be allowed to go out into the terminal and purchase Russian nesting dolls for my kids for Christmas as a memento of this drama.

I did not do my research ahead of time to hear what customers had to say about this particular airline. They have one of the lowest ratings of any airline and habitually cancel flights if the planes are not filled to capacity, without any prior notice. They force passengers to miss connecting flights (and pay for new ones out of their own pocket). Had I known, I would have concluded that the savings were not worth the risk. After two days, they finally scheduled a connecting flight to China and released us from our "prison."

This ordeal resulted in one of those life experiences that will remain embedded in our minds, one that made us laugh heartily later on. But more importantly, it illustrated how travel can force uncomfortable situations onto you, making you flex your adaptability muscles and learn to roll with things.

Flexibility is a quality that enables you to bend easily without breaking. It helps you adapt to situational demands and balance life's demands. A person needs this trait in order to cope with changes in circumstance and to think about solutions and tasks in a novel, creative way. Independent travel brings these situations home more so than most things in life.

When we traveled abroad we did not learn to speak the language, over and above phrases and key words gleaned from the guidebooks. It was nice to learn at least a few words of pleasant exchanges and questions to ask. Locals appreciated our efforts. When we cycled the Camino de Santiago across Spain, we crossed through four different languages in one country: French, Basque, Spanish, and Galician. That would have been a challenge to learn all four for that one trip. Fortunately, English is readily spoken throughout the world, especially where tourists travel, but certainly not everywhere. Often, young people can speak English if a translator is needed. Still, not being able to communicate definitely had its drawbacks, especially in a country like China. There we traveled to destinations away from the normal flow of tourists. The unfamiliar writing system made navigating even more challenging, as illustrated on our excursion across the country on the night train.

TRAINS IN CHINA

Sierra's then-boyfriend, Eben, had found a program to translate English into Chinese characters. Our paper supposedly read, "I want four tickets—hard sleeper beds, on the night train from Xi'an to Beijing." We brought the print-out to the station and received the tickets. It worked successfully for the first leg, Mien Yang to Xi'an.

When Sierra and I went back to the station to purchase the second set of tickets, we stood in a sluggish line for over an hour only to find out we had been in the wrong one. When we finally reached the clerk in the right line, we learned that the tickets for our destination were not available until the following day. The next morning we returned, but the clerk shook her head "no" and pointed to 2 p.m. on her watch. This should have been an omen. On our third try at 2 p.m., she just shook her head "no" again. Sierra then had a verbal fit, although no one could understand what she was saying. The clerk finally brought out the manager who also could not speak English, but Sierra made it clear that we wanted tickets. The manager finally handed them over.

We arrived at the station at 11 p.m. with our huge backpacks, heavy suitcases, and day packs. After piling in what we thought was the sleeper train, we discovered that our designated car had seats. "Where are the beds?" I asked, stunned. "We are supposed to have beds. We bought beds. We must be in the wrong car."

The attendants could not speak English; no one in the car could. Not only were there no beds, but every single seat was filled, including the ones that coincided with the numbers printed on our tickets. The train lurched forward, which immediately made me motion sick. Bundled in a down jacket, hat, scarf, and gloves, with eighty pounds of luggage weighing me down, I felt like I might faint. People wanted to go by but we were standing there, dumbfounded, hogging up the entire aisle. Todd was willing to quietly accept his fate and announced that he was going to go stand by the door *for thirteen hours,* wearing multiple

Nine-month-old Sierra loves camping with her Mama and sleeping in a tent.

(Above) Todd takes his turn caring for little Sierra on a backpacking trip in the Desert Southwest.

(Left) Pre-llama days, each carrying a child on a day hike.

Our string of pack llamas on the Colorado Trail.

Three-year-old Sierra confidently leads her llama, Berrick, down the trail.

Happily picking wildflowers in the Cochetopa Hills of Colorado.

Give Bryce a drawing tool and he is happy, no matter where he is.

Is there anything more fun for a child
than slopping in a creek?

The llama family in Glacier National Park.

Tandem Mountain Biking across New Mexico on the Great Divide Mountain Bike Trail.

Sierra makes friends in the Swiss Alps.

Todd and Sierra have fun riding an elephant in Thailand's Hill Tribe country.

Struggling across the windy plains on Spain's Camino de Santiago.

Sierra cooking on a cook stove at Pennsylvania's Goshenhoppen Festival.

Bryce delivering ice at the Goshenhoppen Festival.

(Above) Enjoying breakfast in the sand dunes of Erg Chebbi, Morocco

(Left) Bryce riding a camel on an overnight Moroccan adventure.

Connecting with new Moroccan friends during a memorable homestay.

Cindy making friends with Katmandu's Hindu Sadhu (holy men) in Nepal.

(Above) Having fun with
Grandmom Ross.

(Right) Taking samples and
measurements of Kentucky's elk
herd with wildlife biologists.

Posing with his inner city buddies at Baun Art Camp, Wyoming, Bryce found a great sense of community.

Sierra is dwarfed by the massive Annapurna Range in Nepal on her and Bryce's solo circumnavigation.

Bryce and Sierra in Patagonia's Los Glaciares National Park.

Camping on a wooden chickie on the 100-mile Wilderness Trail in Florida's Everglades National Park.

Bryce staring down the cables at his mother, as she climbs the side of Half Dome on a rainy Yosemite day.

Bryce taking in glorious Half Dome from Cloud's Rest, Yosemite National Park.

Bringing in the apple harvest at the family's Red Mountain homestead.

The log home that Cindy and Todd built with their own hands.

Cindy and Todd after the kids are grown and on their own.

backpacks. "Don't be ridiculous," I said, but I personally felt as though I could unravel.

I did not let up with my banter and inquiries until finally, an entire family rose out of their seats, with their baby, and silently left. They had high-jacked our seats, but there was no place to put our luggage. The overhead racks were full of overflowing bags and coats, so we propped the backpacks at our feet and in the aisle.

It was incomprehensible to me that we would not have beds for the next thirteen hours. I never sleep on airplanes, even traveling for two days and nights straight, for I am a sensitive, light sleeper. The train seats were arranged in pods and faced one another. The overhead lights, bright as an operating room, remained on all night. I had already taken two motion sickness tablets to knock me out, but the only state I was in was delirious exhaustion.

A jostling cart was pushed down the aisle every half hour, selling all kinds of food, including a Chinese favorite—chicken feet. We stared as they tore open the plastic wrap and pulled out the pale, boiled feet with wrinkly skin. Those who partook inserted the toes in their mouths, clamped down with their teeth, and scraped off what little meat was on it. Then they spit out the toe nails.

Sleep never came the entire night. I was grateful for a bit of people-watching to entertain me, even if it was chicken-feet-eating. Bryce was awake too but had a much better attitude as he spent his hours writing a lengthy, humorous rap about the experience.

On China's night train, I, the mother, the parent, considered having a meltdown. Meltdowns don't happen just to children. Todd had his moment in Rome, where we spent a few days before heading to Sicily to find our relatives. There were "too many people" in Rome, too many expenses, and too much stress for his liking. Out of the blue, only four days into a month-long trip, Todd packed his pack and made an announcement to the family that he was leaving us and going home. Of course, he did not. We gave him a pep talk and assured him things would change as soon as we left the city behind. It was at times like this when we just had to suck it up if we couldn't do anything about the situation. In both of these incidents—crazy, crowded Rome and the Chinese night train—an attitude adjustment and flexibility was called for.

When you travel independently on a long trip, it is difficult to plan out an entire schedule, especially with a complicated itinerary and multiple connections. Stress is bound to enter into the equation. On the flip side, a lot can be said for surprises, spontaneity, serendipity, for meeting new people and having new opportunities. There were times where we changed course en route, resulting in some of our family's fondest memories.

But with independence comes responsibility. There is no tour guide to pass the buck to if a poor choice is made. Being uncomfortable or inconvenienced is certainly possible, and a bad decision could place you in jeopardy. That is not a good thing when it comes to caring for a family of children, but it still happens. I am a little more reckless than Todd, so he reigns me in at times. Todd is timid other times and I push him to take more chances. It's a good balance. The combination has created an adventurous life for the kids, yet a fairly safe one. Sometimes, we don't have all the information when it comes to making choices and we do the best with what we have. How you move around a country can be one of the more challenging aspects of independent travel. In Sicily, we explored the island via bus and one time it left us stranded.

BUSES IN SICILY

We walked the streets of the Sicilian town of Scopello, looking for potential "stealth" camping spots. "Keep your eyes open for a place to sleep tonight," Todd and I announced to our group of family and friends, who had sleeping bags and tents stuffed in their backpacks. We were traveling by bus around the island and had come to this town where the beautiful Zingaro Nature Reserve was located. Sleeping was not on our radar when we unloaded from the bus early in the day. We assumed the national park would offer camping and lodging would be available in town.

This first reserve in Sicily features hiking trails with stunning, open views of the turquoise sea. From the high, exposed white cliffs the footpaths dipped down to pebbly beaches ringing the Tyrrhenian Sea. After hiking all day, we discovered that there were no campgrounds, and that all the hotels were filled. In addition, no buses would be entering or leaving town until the next morning. We had not done our homework. We were stuck. An abandoned pizzeria on a hillside looked promising.

We waited until dusk fell and then creeped up the one-way gravel road that looped around the property to the restaurant's patio. The hillside was rural, with scattered homes on the outskirts of town. The pizzeria looked like it might have been thriving only a few years ago. We quietly scraped away the glass shards and trash with our feet, righted the white plastic stackable chairs and set up our tents, as the mosquitos came out in force. Every time someone unzipped a tent fly, the neighborhood dogs would bark. The kids giggled as silently as they could.

Down the road was a nice restaurant, with white linen tablecloths and napkins and three crystal glasses at each place setting. We ordered pizza. The kids whispered, "We're living like the homeless, but eating like the rich. This is great!"

After dinner, we kept our headlamps off and walked in darkness back to the abandoned pizzeria. The plan was that Todd would sleep outside the tent and rouse us at the first crack of light. We would pack up and leave before anyone knew of our presence. However, in the early grey morning, Todd was wildly awoken by the crunching of tires on the gravel. Someone was coming up the drive and, they were shooting a gun! A car spun by and Todd saw the figure of a man rising out of the rear car window, with a rifle in his hand. He was taking aim, and firing.

The gunman never saw us. He was too intent on seeking small game, rats, other trespassers, or who knows what. The car circled the pizzeria, the backseat passenger shooting away, and then rocketed down the other side of the gravel loop. Afterwards, it took twenty minutes for Todd's knees to stop shaking, as he witnessed the whole event while the rest of us slept peacefully. We tore down the tent in a flash and slithered out to the road. The kids gave us a high five when we reached the blacktop public road and announced, "That was *the best* night of the whole trip."

Todd was still in shock from what had just occurred. Sierra and Bryce seemed to take situations like this in stride. They saw it as an adventure. We later read in the *Rough Guide*'s description of Scopello that the town had one of the worst reputations in Sicily for Mafia violence in the 1950s. Eighty percent of the adult males had served prison sentences and one in three had committed murder.

Another family, who weren't backpackers, would have needed to reach out and ask for help. They might have knocked on doors and somehow overcame the language barrier, as they searched for a willing homeowner who had the extra beds, for a price. We had the necessary gear to take care of the situation on our own. If the car with the gunman had never driven up the road that morning and we packed up without incident, it would have been a quiet, uneventful stay. If we were part of a tour group and not traveling independently, "the best night in Sicily" would not have happened.

Early in their childhood, Sierra and Bryce accepted the fact that life will not always go their way or as planned. They learned this as they were buffeted by storms on the Continental Divide, when they arrived at wide riverbanks with no bridges, or came around the bend to a trail swallowed in late season snow with no visible way through. There will be many times in the course of one's life when difficulties and obstacles will arise. It is important to remain calm, think rationally, explore options, and use creativity to solve problems.

We did not travel independently with the purpose of seeking out episodes that would test our flexibility. We traveled for fun, to grow and learn. Learning flexibility as well as the importance of a positive attitude, was a welcomed byproduct. Foreign countries are a great arena to practice this skill since so much is left to chance. If you do not possess flexibility before you began to travel abroad independently, it will be forced upon you.

TREKKING IN NEPAL (THE PARENTS)

When we decided to stretch ourselves and go trekking in Nepal's Himalaya mountains, we were hoping we could do it independently, without a guide. A good friend had trekked there multiple times, so he gave us excellent advice on how to do it.

We chose a weeklong trek up the Langtang Valley. We would travel in one direction until we pierced the high mountains; then we would turn around and retrace our steps back out. Simple and difficult to get lost. We planned to stay at inexpensive guest houses so we did not need to bring a tent, sleeping bags or pads, or very much food. Our day packs were light.

Every foreigner we saw had a guide and a porter, however. Granted, they were inexpensive—$10 a day for a guide and $10 a day for a porter, at the time. Hiring was encouraged but we didn't want someone attached at our hip, spending every waking moment with us.

When we encountered other tourists, they all asked where our guide was. "That would be me," I said as I studied the data from our trekking guidebook and the map. Then they asked, "Where is your porter?"

"That would be me," Todd replied, laughing.

Being in charge of our trek left a lot up to chance too so we had to practice rolling with the adventures, while staying flexible.

The adventure began before we even reached the mountains, as the bus ride to the head of the Langtang Valley gave us ten full hours of lifelong memories. Todd and I scored seats right by the entrance and were grateful for the fresh air the opening door brought in. It also brought in mamas and their babies. Two of the mothers plopped their small children onto Todd's lap before they even climbed completely aboard. No words were exchanged. The children remained there for hours. One little boy draped his arms lovingly around Todd's neck.

A man got on with a tumpline across his forehead, holding up a massive woven basket of onions. A crate of ducks was placed under a seat and a huge box of cherry tomatoes blocked the step leading into the bus. Every passenger had to be helped over it as the stretch was wide.

One woman just planted her foot right into the tomatoes on purpose, to hell with it. A goat was thrown into the back of the bus, tied and crying as the bus bounced along the rutted road. The bus got so crowded that people leaned into Todd and the one closest to him puked all over his shoulder and back. Although you can hire a private SUV transport, which is a few hours faster and considerably more money, a trekker would miss this cultural experience. Here was real gritty Nepali life—local bus culture. After this, Todd and I had a new reference point on what a "long, hard bus ride" was, even though we opted for the expensive SUV ride back out, we are glad to have done it at least once in life.

The culture along the Langtang Valley trail was captivating. Himalayan people walked up and down the same valley trail, carrying great loads of sticks. Some herded goats and cows; others walked spinning handheld, silver prayer wheels. The route led us right through their yards and patios, descending their steps, as we stopped at little family-run tea shops perched on the cliffside trail. Yaks grazed in the meadows, and women in colorful traditional clothing plowed the land.

In every tiny village and establishment, there were guest homes, offering meals and lodging. The price was equivalent to only a few dollars and overnight was sometimes free if we purchased dinner and breakfast. We didn't need prior reservations; everyone wanted our business and we had our pick of places. We befriended one family and stayed with the owner's other two sisters in higher villages. They welcomed us like family when we told them who had sent us. The flexibility we earned by planning as we trekked gave us many more unplanned, wonderful experiences.

TREKKING IN NEPAL (THE KIDS)

The first adventure Sierra and Bryce chose as independent travelers was an epic backpacking trip of their own, also in the Himalayas. Sierra was doing a semester abroad in Nepal during her junior year of college and so it was the perfect opportunity for her and Bryce to stretch their wings and attempt a trek in these iconic mountains. Our children hiked the Annapurna Circuit, which circles one of the highest peaks on the planet, Annapurna. This two-week trek takes the hiker up to 17,769 feet in elevation. Nineteen-year-old Bryce was nervous about navigating alone through the airports of Russia and India, and spending a night in the Delhi airport. He had to pass through security, which in India can be intimidating, acquire a visa upon landing in Nepal, and resort to charades when asking for help from people who could not speak English.

After Bryce arrived in Katmandu, his trip began when he was whisked away to the mountains on a nauseating ten-hour bus ride, like Todd and I, before he could recuperate from jet lag. Bryce made it an even bigger adventure by riding on the bus roof with young Nepalese, some of whom were drunk and falling off. Teenagers ducked under electric lines, lifting them up with wooden sticks so that the bus could pass along the narrow, rutted roads.

On the trek, Sierra chose to bring along a heavy gruel of roasted barley flour called *tsampa* that Tibetans and other Himalayan people eat, mixing it with hot butter tea. She threw about ten pounds of it into her brother's pack (unbeknownst to him) which he hauled all around Annapurna. It was way too heavy and grew unappetizing quickly and hence not a good choice as trekker food. Had Todd and I accompanied them, we would have never selected a ten-pound bag of tsampa, but they were in the process of learning what works and what doesn't work on their own.

Of his time in Nepal, Bryce wrote:

Sierra and I had to learn how to deal with uncomfortable situations, coping with altitude sickness, bargaining for prices, deciding who to trust, i.e. the 'child' bus driver who nearly got us killed on our way to the Himalayas. However, my past experiences taught me to be adaptable, in whatever situation I found myself in. Multiple times I drew on what I had learned from my family's travels, remembering how Mom had gotten us through tricky situations. Although I had been young, I was observing and learning subconsciously, and had not realized how much information I could draw on in a time of need. It was a rewarding challenge, to circumnavigate Annapurna without the leadership of our parents, to test ourselves and see if we could do it. Afterwards we got nose and ear piercings to celebrate our rite of passage!

After Sierra and Bryce successfully completed the Annapurna circuit, a surprising discovery was made, by Sierra's then-boyfriend, Eben. He was reading my sixth book, *Scraping Heaven*, when he came across this excerpt in the epilogue. The kids were ten and twelve years old at the time of my writing: "Todd and I figure we may only have a few years left before Sierra will resist missing out on something back home, so we have the next few major trips planned. But other adventuring families have told me teenagers don't mind making exotic trips with their families. After all, how long will it be before Sierra and Bryce can afford to trek the Himalaya or hike the Annapurna Circuit with their friends?"

I used the Annapurna Circuit as an example of high independent adventure, because at the time, it seemed completely far-fetched and absurd. Our family had done little traveling abroad at that point and a Himalayan trek was not on my radar.

I had completely forgotten that I had ever penned those words. Todd read them aloud to twelve-year-old Sierra before she went to bed. We thought they had left her mind. Instead, they must have planted a seed.

NUTS AND BOLTS

STUDENT EXCHANGE

If a student does not have parents who can afford the time or the expense or who do not have the interest to take their children abroad, there are opportunities to bring foreign children into your family life. These experiences teach how to adapt and embrace a foreign culture and people, setting children up for a life of independent travel as adults.

Rotary International is an organization that creates and supports services that advance goodwill and peace around the world, amongst other missions. They have chapters all over the world that offer short and long-term exchange programs. Rotary International also sponsors a full academic year abroad for high school students and only charges families the flight fee, as opposed to other student exchange programs that may also charge tuition or boarding fees. After Sierra's senior year of high school, she did a Rotary exchange with an Ecuadorian girl. Sierra went to Ande's home town of Riobamba for three weeks and then afterwards, Ande came to our home for three weeks. It felt very scary for Sierra to take that first step out into the world on her own, inserting herself into a strange family with a different culture and a language challenge on top of it. But it proved to be a very positive experience, in both directions of the exchange, showing Ande her world in Pennsylvania and also learning to fit into an Ecuadorian world. Through it, Sierra gained the confidence to study abroad in college for an entire semester.

Our family's summer exchange program was very short. Exchanges lasting an entire school year can reap even more benefits. Our friends, the Hollidays, did not want to raise their only child, Davis, insulated from other cultures but hoped to broaden his understanding of other people. When Davis was in sixth grade, Matt and Tracy brought over a German boy who attended their local school for a nine-month period and was embraced as a member of their family. Through the experience, their son learned how to interact with another child on a daily basis in his home, as if he had a sibling. Their first exchange was so successful that they brought three more students over during Davis's middle-high school years.

Although our American friends acted as hosts, their son never personally spent his school year abroad. The cost to the family sending their child was an estimated $10,000, which mainly goes to the school district, insurance, and flights. Although the host family supplies food and some travel experiences, it costs far less to host than sending your child abroad. It is a viable option for an exchange to only go one way if a family cannot afford to send their own child abroad or if their child does not want to go. Student exchange is a very viable alternative if a family wants to experience a foreign culture but does not travel far and for a long period of time themselves.

Another way to get your son or daughter to experience a foreign culture could be through their university on a Service Immersion Program. Temple University, where both Sierra and Bryce attended, offers week-long programs to the South Dakota Rosebud Reservation of the Sioux/Lakota tribe. These native people are truly a separate nation with their own customs, language, and history. Very little money is required from the student as fund-raising is part of the program.

There are opportunities available to WWOOF (World Wide Opportunities on Organic Farms). This loose network of national organizations offers opportunities to live, work, and learn as volunteers, all over the world. No money is exchanged, but work services are only required for a half-day and the WWOOFer is free to explore the locale for the rest of the time. This unique educational opportunity helps build a global community and spread the knowledge of ecological farming practices.

There are also many volunteer opportunities available worldwide. Explore them through websites like www.volunteerforever.com, www.globalvolunteers.org, and www.volunteerworld.com. Young people can find opportunities to teach English abroad too for a semester or a year. Check out www.goabroad.com and www.transitionabroad.com.

We live in an increasingly globalized world where our young people will need to interact with, communicate with, and understand people of other cultures, histories, and languages. There will always be issues to work on that know no borders, like curing diseases, finding energy solutions, and fighting terrorism and hunger. Travel abroad pushes young people out of their comfort zone early and helps them appreciate diversity firsthand. They will see stereotypes that they may have held about other cultures, and then hopefully dismiss them and work toward building bridges.

International study and travel abroad has become a necessity in many leadership roles and jobs, especially those involving business and trade. If parents cannot afford to take their children, they can seek assistance. Two important organizations that can help the student with aid and finding opportunities are ISEP (International Student Exchange Program) and SYTA (Student and Youth Travel Association).

The Peace Corps recently ran an electronic ad that summed up the importance of exposing ourselves to other cultures and people.

"Make America a Better Place—Leave the Country. Some do not think you can change the world through the Peace Corps. On the other hand, maybe it's not just what you do in the Peace Corps that counts, but what you do when you get back."

The truth is, we become transformed when we have international experiences, into life-long learners who are broad-minded, accepting, flexible adults. The following short essay, by seventeen-year-old Sierra, written for her Rotary Exchange Program application, is a good example of its positive impact.

I am who I am because of my life. My education is my life and my life is my education. It is absolutely impossible for me to separate the two. I learn from whatever I do. What I do in my free time is what I do for school. And whatever I am learning about at the time is what I love.

I don't remember when I started to learn. It is lost in the recesses of my mind—a young child on the back of a llama, gazing at the great, wild undeveloped vastness of our country. There is so much out there: so many things to smell and taste, so many animals disappearing, so many ancient cities haunted by the ghosts of civilization. I want to know it all. I want to think every idea. I want to know the hands that shaped and sculpted who we are today. I want to know the world. I am going to spend the rest of my life learning.

CHAPTER 8

Learning from Our Ancestors

"If you become a bird and fly away from me," said his
mother, "I will be a tree that you come home to."
Margaret Wise Brown, *The Runaway Bunny*

SICILY

*"Driving the narrow country roads into Delia, I look out across the olive
groves and vineyards and think—this is the land of my ancestors."*—Fifteen-
year-old Sierra

My parents died long before I became a mother, both at the young age
of fifty-seven. Many are the times I wished I could travel back and share
them with my children. The things they could teach Sierra and Bryce
would be endless and priceless and provide a window into the past.

There were some local ancestors alive on my father's side while my children were growing up—Sierra and Bryce's great Aunt Dot Lachina and great grandmother Anna Ross—but not on my mother's side. My mother's brothers died at an even younger age, both from failing hearts. We would need to travel back to Sicily if we wanted to learn more, so that is what we did. For the same amount of money that an all-inclusive resort vacation would cost, we were able to return to my Sicilian ancestor's homeland and give my children a life-changing experience. Sierra and Bryce could experience real Sicilians, learn about their heritage, and shed some light on who they are.

After we did research on locating my ancestors abroad, we attempted contact. Unless your relatives are savvy young people (who speak English and are connected to the Internet) who care about their American relatives, you may be on your own. You could just travel back to your ancestors' village in the homeland and begin to ask questions, which is basically what we did, but we had fortune on our side and a strange twist of fate. In the small village of Delia where my mother's family, the Borzellinos, hailed from, there was also another very dominant family who populated the area, the Lachinas.

Back in America, my mother, Grace Borzellino, married a Pole, Joe Ross, whom she met in Reading, Pennsylvania. My father's sister, Dorothy Ross, also a Pole, of course, married another Sicilian, Ignatius Lachina. *His* family also hailed from the same small Sicilian village as my mother's, Delia, although the two families in America did not know one another. When Todd, Sierra, Bryce, and I traveled to Sicily and walked the streets of Delia looking for our ancestors, we realized that nearly everyone in Delia was either a Lachina or a Borzellino. "Hey! You my cousin!" they greeted us, and it was remarkably true. With the town's help, we were able to find our immediate Borzellino family, first cousins to my mother.

Sierra, November 2005:

As soon as we step into the door of our relatives' homes in Delia, Sicily, they throw their arms around us and pepper our faces with kisses.

Unbeknownst to us, they've been communicating with the Lachinas and have been talking about our visit for months, and the entire family comes over to meet us—generation after generation streaming in the door. They all line up to make their rounds and we just stand there as each one pecks both our cheeks. Unfortunately, we were not warned that you are supposed to kiss from left to right, so many jaws were whacked. Our interpreter, a woman named Providence, flounders to keep up with introductions. Before long the tiny kitchen is crammed with people, kissing, hugging, and squeezing by. Everyone is talking in Italian, tracing back the generations to where our blood pools together. The sound is deafening, everyone talking over each other and the volume rising higher and higher like the crescendo of an orchestra with everyone conducting with flamboyant hand gestures.

While this is happening, our hosts are plopping heaping plates of pasta in front of us and sawing off huge hunks of bread and pouring us drinks and grating parmesan cheese onto our noodles. Little kids are under the table playing peekaboo and the kitchen is packed like a tin of sardines and louder than a school cafeteria. I just sit there eating spaghetti, laughing in disbelief. I look over at my mom and finally get why she behaves the way she does.

We asked our relatives if we could participate in the olive harvest while we were visiting to connect a little deeper with this Sicilian way of life. Some members of my family have olive oil manufacturing/bottling plants and distribute oil as a business; others have their own personal grove for their family's oil use, much like how we Americans grow tomatoes in the back yard.

Out in the grove, we beat the upper branches of the olive trees with long sticks which made the olives fall like pouring rain. With hand rakes, we combed through the lower branches as though we were brushing Rapunzel's hair. The hard, little balls, light green in color with an occasional dark brown spot, or half and half as they were just ripening, collected onto the mesh tarps spread beneath the trees. We poured the tarp's contents into feed bags and hauled them down to the neighbor-hood olive press.

The air inside the building was thick with a green mist. The con-crete floor was slick with oil. The olives were dumped into vats that vibrated to remove their leaves, and then inched down a conveyor belt to be ground into a thick greasy paste. The pulp was compacted, the dark water siphoned off and the emerald green oil was tapped into plastic casts. Here was the nectar of our ancestors, the food that sustained us.

Except for the olive harvest, most of our short stay in Delia revolved around locating more relatives. We took an English-speaking friend of the family along as an interpreter and translator and were rewarded with finding many cousins.

Sierra wrote:

It is amazing to find pieces of Mom sprinkled about in all the differ-ent families. One cute little lady has the exact prominent jaw; another had the same shaped nose. One cousin even has the same monstrous thighs peeking out from under her hem.

I get goose bumps as we sit around the cozy kitchens tracking back the generations and uttering the names of my ancestors aloud. I can feel their spirits tingling in the air, an electric buzz of excitement as someone remembers a story, a name. There is definitely power here as we piece together the family tree. It's like solving a puzzle—solving the mystery of our past, of who we truly are.

But the most touching relative we meet is a little old woman named Graziella, a cousin of my grandmother's. This shrunken little old lady with round bugging eyes, pale powdery skin, stands on her tiptoes to kiss our cheeks. She lives all alone in an empty house that was once my great-grandfather's.

My flesh prickles as I step through the door. I scan the ceiling, the walls. There is a picture of Graziella as a young woman and she looks exactly like the ones I've seen of my grandmother.

Graziella is so overtaken with happiness to find relatives when she thought she was alone that she takes my mom by the arm and leads her over to the faded black and white portraits of her parents hanging on the wall. Voice shaking and eyes watering, she begins praying and thanking her parents in Italian for bringing us to her. My heart has risen so far up in my throat I have to swallow. Everyone is crying. By the time we leave, we have a whole new family. It's amazing that we've only been in Delia for forty-eight hours. I feel like I've known everyone my whole life!

This experience of going back to find my roots left me feeling like I understood at least a small part of where I came from. Your past is what makes you who you are, all your experiences, your mistakes, the lessons you've learned. But digging deeper, you can understand what went into making you. Tracing back your roots is like tracing back the thread that connects you to your family, to people, to the world, to the great web of life.

I think it is important for others, especially teenagers to go back and find where they came from. It gives you a sense of understanding and confidence of who you are. Roots—they give you a solid foundation to grow from.

As teenagers make the transition from child to adult, it is often a struggle to understand and become your own person. Often, we attempt to sever the bonds with our families and break free, when establishing strong, hearty ties are a necessity. When it comes down to it, shoots can't grow without their roots. How else can we grow to become our own beautiful and independent tree?

It was a remarkable experience as a mother, to observe all this through my children's eyes, but what also struck us was Todd's reaction to this rapid and intense encounter. His German/Swiss demeanor is naturally private, guarded, and quiet. He does not indulge in an outward show of affection by choice. Yet his eyes welled with tears as he hugged and kissed everyone good-bye. We can learn to be demonstrative in our feelings even if that is not our usual behavior. Love knows no boundaries. Love like this always feels good.

It was interesting to see that the amount of love exchanged amongst family had nothing to do with the amount of time spent with them or how long you actually know them. In this case, it was a mere forty-eight hours. Now Sierra and Bryce understood the reserved private German side of their father's family and the affectionate, outgoing Sicilian side of their mother's. Knowing who came before them gave them a glimpse into who they are today and what a gift at thirteen and fifteen years old.

About the time we returned home from Sicily, it dawned on me that my ninety-nine-year-old Polish Grandmom Anna Ross would not live for *too* many more years. What were we waiting for? Spending quality time with her was as close to an ancestor's homeland as we could get. We felt certain there was a lot she could teach us. Sierra, Bryce, and I began to make frequent trips to nearby Reading to take Grandmom on outings and share simple times with her, at an age when most young teens would not think of hanging out with an elderly person by choice.

It didn't matter what activity we were doing, embroidering pillow cases at her knee, rolling dough out to fry homemade fastnachts, playing BINGO! or going on car drives, it was her stories, her behavior, that Sierra and Bryce soaked up and marveled at. She told them stories of how her sixteen-year-old parents met on a ship coming from Europe— her mother from Germany, her father from Poland. Her mother gave birth to sixteen children and had to quit school in the fourth grade to help support the family by ironing clothes for rich people.

One day, when she was fourteen, my grandmother watched her sixty-four-year-old mother lie down in her bed. She asked, "Aren't you gonna get up, Mama?"

Her mother replied, "No, I'm so tired," and died, leaving Grandmom to go to work washing dishes.

"I got three dollars a week washing dishes from 7 a.m. to 7 p.m." When Sierra and Bryce looked at her aghast she admitted, "I thought it was normal."

Her husband, Joe, died in his mid-fifties and for almost fifty years, she lived alone, outliving all of her siblings and most of her children. She was the landlady of her apartment house in a rough section of Reading, Pennsylvania. Her daughter, my Aunt Dot, wanted to see her live somewhere safer with company, but it had been her home for over fifty years, and she had always been fine there. In her elderly years, a man bleeding from gunshots crawled into her vestibule and woke her up one night. Another evening she was startled awake by thieves trying to pry her stained-glass transom window out of her front door. Both times she simply dialed 911. Fear never entered into the equation.

She told Sierra and Bryce these stories, laughing, over a hand of 500 rummy in her yellow painted kitchen with a bowl of ice cream. Both children listened wide-eyed, imagining what the scene must have looked like. She taught us not to be afraid of life by her own fearless example.

On our drives, she looked around and marveled at everything—a dormitory at a local college, a line of puff-chested, white doves on a wire. I glanced in the rearview mirror and watched the kids searching for what Grandmom thought was so beautiful as we passed by and invariably got that open-mouth-gape that I got as a child (my father used to ask if I was catching flies), thinking deeply, looking hard.

At the cemetery where my parents are buried, she exclaimed, "Look how all the gravestones are so beautifully lined up!"

And the kids whispered, "Grandmom sees beauty everywhere!" Yes, and everything is a gift—my grandmother is very powerful medicine to be around, as the Native Americans would say.

When we shared a meal with her, she would cast her eyes up to heaven, or to a nearby picture of Jesus, tear up, and say, "Thank you for bringing my wonderful family to me." It completely amazed my kids, that a one or two-hour visit could move someone to tears. When we entered her home, she cupped our faces in her wrinkled, spotted hands and said, "You are a sight for sore eyes!" She taught us the great gift of gratitude.

When we were all in the car one day, I became frustrated driving behind a slow vehicle. She said, "It's okay, Cindy, we have all the time in the world." How absurd, I thought, for her to say that. At nearly one hundred years old, she was running out of time! But she lived as though she had all the time in the world.

Like so many people in their mid-life, I lived with a sense of urgency. I drove quickly between errands, growing impatient behind slowpokes, cramming as many activities into a day as possible. "Move quickly and move often" was my mantra. But when someone offers her arm to a one-hundred-year-old, she does not exactly zip along.

Sierra and Bryce had to slow down too in her company and cater to her. They opened her car door, offered their arms, let her lean on them, and walked her pace. She taught us all to slow down.

On the way home that day after our cemetery visit, the kids had questions about death and dying. They wanted full-blown details on how my parents died; one slow and wasting away from cancer, and the other one quickly from a heart attack. They wanted to know what experiencing death was like, and I told them how amazing it was to watch the transformation when a person's spirit leaves their body, leaving behind a shell, a house that is no longer needed, and how I came to realize that we are not our bodies. They had questions on burials, cremation, and what I thought might happen in the afterlife. My children were thinking, asking important questions, all prompted by being in the presence of a centenarian, who was a lot closer to death than they were.

On one of my last visits before she died, she saw my hair tied back revealing my temples and said, "Why, Cindy, I believe you're getting gray."

"No, Grandmom, I'm getting white, but I'm not ready to dye it yet."

A little hard of hearing, she replied, "Oh, I'm not ready to die yet either!" She was truly too busy living to think about dying.

She infected her daughter, my Aunt Dot, with the same zest for life. Aunt Dot skydived and zip-lined for the first time in her seventies. In her early eighties, she whitewater rafted class-3, with the whole family of four generations coming together for the celebratory paddle.

"I don't feel like I'm old," she told Sierra and Bryce. "I feel like a teenager."

Besides being a spectacular inspiration, my grandmother's 102 years of life stood as testimony of her belief that people have a choice whether or not they want to be happy in life. There are benefits to seeking beauty and living in a constant state of gratitude—perhaps this attitude contributed to creating a long and happy life.

Volunteering at a retirement community, assisted living, or a senior center is an easy way to bring the wisdom, fun, and history of our elders into our own lives. Learning from those who have lived for a long time is an invaluable gift. It brings our own lives and challenges into perspective, and if we choose to listen, we will hear a history lesson every day. For a few years, I served as a hospice volunteer. My new, yet short-lived, friends taught me volumes about this gift of life—to not be afraid of passing, but see it as a natural and expected part of life.

POLAND

When twenty-three-year-old Sierra explored ideas of which country to visit with her mother to celebrate her graduation from Temple University, Poland rose to the top of her list. Our family's remarkable visit to Sicily eight years before made such a lasting impact, Sierra longed to return to the other side of her mother's family and learn more about her Polish ancestors.

In 1907, my Polish grandfather, Joe Raszewski, sailed across the ocean to America with his twelve-year-old sister, Catharine, who was terribly young to have been in charge of her little brother on such an arduous journey. In Poland, their parents had just passed away, most likely from severe illness. They were born in a log cabin in the rural village of Wesola in southwest Poland. Joe and Catharine would have also died had it not been for a generous aunt in Philadelphia who sponsored their emigration to America.

When our taxi driver left us off outside the looming brick building in Krosno, "Uncle" Tadek and "Aunt" Bogusha unlocked the gate and flung open their arms to embrace us as we laid eyes on one another for the first time. It was magical. They talked entirely in Polish and of course, we did not understand a single word. But their thirty-six-year-old pilot son, Andrzej, was there to translate.

The table was set for dinner: pirogues, kielbasa, red beet soup, rye bread, and other traditional Polish food. Course after course arrived while we looked at old photos and Andrzej listened and then translated.

Tadek's mother, my grandfather's sister, returned to Poland with a husband and raised her family here. My grandfather remained in America and built his family there. As we talked, I was startled to realize that there were things about his face that looked so much like my own father's, his first cousin—the shape of his full lips, his hazel eyes, and his distinct bumped nose. I started to blink back tears, for I have so missed my wonderful father in the last thirty-five years. It was as if he had come back to life.

One of my goals while in Poland was to try to locate the actual log home that my grandfather was born in. Since we also live in a log home that Todd and I built by hand, I thought the connection remarkable. If we could find it, if it indeed still existed, after over one hundred years, it would be nothing short of a miracle.

I always felt akin to my Polish grandmother, Anna. She had said that Pop Pop, my grandfather, had loved to travel, for indeed it began when he was only four on his trip to America. He had been a bit of a renegade, knew what he wanted in life and wasn't afraid to take chances to get it. I hoped I inherited some of his spirit.

The day Sierra and I traveled forty kilometers with our relatives, in search of my grandfather's log home, was the most memorable. There was no road sign announcing the turn to Wesola, for the village was so small. We were looking for a low, one-story, blue-painted log home with the number 636 on it that we saw in an old photo. But it could have been framed over, renovated, or even demolished.

After a long search, we found number 635, a brick home, and traveled across the drive to the back. Just as we were getting ready to knock, only a few yards away, we spied another building, low to the ground, which had been totally hidden from view. "There it is! There's my grandfather's home!" We were completely taken by surprise. It was as if it suddenly materialized out of thin air, willed into existence by our desire to find it.

We took photos and looked at the surrounding land, trying to imagine my great-grandparents coming to this place, drawn to the far-reaching views of rolling hills on each side of the ridge. It reminded Sierra and me of our home in Pennsylvania. We too had built a log home on a ridge, with views of the valley. My ancestors had to have been in touch with the seasons, growing their own food like we do. I tried to imagine my grandfather's mother giving birth in there and then his parents dying in there, and what that must have felt like for those very alone children.

In her journal, Sierra wrote, *"It was interesting to walk through the grass and look out through the small orchard over the hills and imagine my great grandfather as a four-year-old running through the high grass. He probably never remembered much from here but his heart probably still ached for the bliss of being a child before his parents died of sickness and he was orphaned and sent to America in the bowels of a ship with Uncle Tadek's mother, Catherine."*

Cousin Andrzej became our fast friend over these few days as we teased and joked and his sarcastic wit shone through spectacularly. My own father had been an expert at sarcasm, teaching me and all my siblings how to poke fun at the world and its people. It has gotten us into trouble more than a few times with those lacking an appreciation for this type of humor. Andrzej says it is a highly intelligent form of humor and it is our "family's way. It is in our DNA."

Sierra and I felt very connected to this family, who were complete strangers a few days ago, who looked like me and had the same humor. Andrzej said, "I am thirty-six, but I feel twenty-one." I get that. "I am fifty-seven but I feel thirty-one." There are relatives back home who get this too—relatives who ignored their age, like my Aunt Dot, Tadek's first cousin, who skydived, zip-lined, and whitewater rafted in her late seventies to early eighties.

The wonderful visit with our relatives culminated on our last day when Andrzej planned a special outing for Sierra and me. He borrowed three bikes and jammed them into his car, purchased a loop of kielbasa and a loaf of rye bread, and we sped off on a biking adventure.

As we cycled through the forest and meadows, Andrzej yelled back to me, "I love bike riding!" and I just smiled. We do too. We stooped to comb the forest duff for edible orange mushrooms and slit their necks and popped them into a cloth bag for supper. We stopped at a camp and gathered dry dead fir sticks and Andrzej started a fire and sharpened sticks to skewer kielbasa lengths in the sizzling fire. No quick snack of a granola bar with this man.

"Does everyone do this when they go for a bike ride?" we asked.

"Only the crazy ones," he said. The skin of the sausage stretched, allowing the delicious juices to run out and as we sat gnawing our sausage around the crackling fire, we thought, only in Poland, only with our relatives.

As I sat on the bus ride back to the Krakow airport, I continually teared up as I thought of my Polish relatives. What did I expect? As Andrzej said, "It's in the DNA." The love is in the DNA. Andrzej later told me that Wesola, the village of my grandfather, means "happy" in Polish. No wonder our lives have been blessed by abundance. Look at where we have come from.

The amazing thing was that we found pieces of ourselves clear around the world, in tiny villages like Krosno, Poland and Delia, Sicily, places we never knew existed. We found people who had the same facial features and body type as us, who had the same personality traits and humor. And so they loved us even more for we were one of their own.

Even if a person's ancestors are gone from the homeland or are unknown, exploring the land of our relatives gives us connection, and insight into who we are and where we have come from, for who we are is not random. Our genes bear half the responsibility for our diversity. As the Native American poet Linda Hogan said, "We are the result of the love of thousands."

Happy Grandmom Ross died at the ripe old age of 102. She never took any medication. She climbed into bed like her mother did eighty-eight years before her, just because she was tired. She too did not plan to get up. Many of her grandchildren and great grandchildren surrounded her and sang Bobby Vinton Polish songs with her as she drifted off to sleep and passed on.

NUTS AND BOLTS

The best place to begin researching your ancestors is right from the horse's mouth, your living ancestors themselves. Honor and celebrate the living elders you still have. Make the time to share experiences and create memories with them and by all means, bring your children along. Create new family customs and celebrations. Incorporate your elderly relatives into your life, especially those who are house-bound and include them in outings. They will be extremely grateful and everyone will benefit.

As far as locating your relatives in the homeland, even close families are unaware of which relatives possess knowledge/information so reach out to everyone and ask questions. Often second cousins and those farther removed may know something beyond your circle of immediate family. Someone may be way ahead in genealogy research and save you much trouble and work. *Family Tree Magazine* offers articles on the best genealogy websites for beginners.

There has been an explosion of genetic testing that can also help with your search. Exploring the Arrival Records at the Family History

Center at Ellis Island, New York, can be insightful if your relatives immigrated through this port. If all you know is a town in the home-land, it is still worth the trip to your ancestors' country to try to locate relatives. Even if you strike out, much can be learned about your people by traveling there personally and just soaking in the place, especially with your children. You might be surprised to learn that a family trip abroad could compete financially with a vacation at Disneyland.

If you experience one strike-out after another or can't afford to travel abroad to your own family's homeland, join a local social club like the Polish Falcons of America, Irish Club of the Ancient Order of the Hibernians, the Jewish Community Center, the Italian American Social Club, etc. Many ethnic clubs embrace one other as if they were blood family and much can be learned from them about your people.

CHAPTER 9

Learning from Self-Propelled Travel

"You were stubborn . . . and fought against the storm, which proved stronger than you: but we bow and yield to every breeze, and thus the gale passed harmlessly over our heads."

"The Oak and the Reeds," *Aesop's Fables*

BY BICYCLE

THE CAMINO DE SANTIAGO

Light from dozens of burning candles reflected off the ancient church's high vaulted ceilings, while pungent incense filled our nostrils. For eight hundred years, monks at the abbey in Roncevalles, Spain, have been reciting a special blessing to pilgrims as they begin their journey on the Way of St. James, or the Camino de Santiago. My family and I were four of two hundred people starting out across Spain's Iberian Peninsula in 2003. A priest recited each and every one of the countries from which the pilgrims hailed and we elbowed each other when we heard *Estados Unidos*. If we didn't think what we were about to do was monumental, a self-propelled cycling adventure to the mortal remains of Saint James, it slammed us now as our eyes filled with tears.

The journey to Santiago is one of the three great Christian pilgrimages in the world, along with those to Rome and Jerusalem. Regardless of one's personal religious beliefs, the blessings that are bestowed upon pilgrims along the Camino can be very meaningful. Our bike ride on Spain's Camino became one of the most inspiring journeys of our lives.

The day's starting pilgrims were invited up to the altar where five white-robed monks extended their arms above our bowed heads. We came from every corner of the world to this tiny twelfth-century monastery in the foothills of the Pyrenees.

For more than 1,500 years, most pilgrims have walked, carrying a small backpack and a clam shell, the symbol of the Camino, but we chose to cycle the route. We toted between twenty and forty-five pounds of gear, and covered between thirty and forty miles a day. Accommodations were hostel-like shelters and ran the gamut from modern establishments to 1,700-year-old monasteries. We crossed the same rivers on the same ancient bridges as our medieval forbearers. We passed through the same villages, and visited the same chapels, churches, and cathedrals. Every day was a field trip through a continuous museum.

Pilgrims from over sixty countries were represented the year we cycled. They made the journey for historical, cultural, religious, and athletic reasons. We cycled it for a combination of all of the above and simply because we loved to ride bikes. We enjoyed taking self-propelled journeys where we move ourselves and our gear using nothing but the energy from our own muscles.

This style of travel has the potential to teach us much about perseverance. On a self-propelled trip, you might be forced to do something despite difficulty, failure, opposition, or delayed gratification, in order to achieve success. Perseverance gives you the self-control and endurance to work through challenges, whether they are of the mind, the body, or the spirit. It gives you a sense of pride and self-confidence knowing that you tried hard and did your best. In the bigger picture, this trait helps a person work through difficult issues, maintain relationships and develop a good work ethic. In our family's view, a self-propelled adventure is a great way to learn and practice this important trait.

Contrary to our hiking journeys where we saw very few people in the vast wilderness, the Camino was very crowded. The "every man" walks the Camino, including many who are not accustomed to long-distance, self-propelled journeys, so there is real suffering to observe. Old people, out-of-shape people, and people who clearly have never walked any farther than from their car to the store tackle the Camino. The hostels were full of people swabbing their blistered feet with liniments and napping at all hours from exhaustion. It was a cornucopia of different cultures and humans trying to cope with the challenges of the journey.

Sierra and Bryce heard dozens of languages being spoken along the way. They observed how people looked, dressed, and behaved from all parts of the world, all gathered together on one pathway. We cooked side by side with Portuguese people in the hostels, shared a bunk room with Germans, made friends with cycling Brazilians, and met a man from Rome who was pushing his sick wife in a wheelchair across all three of the pilgrim paths. If the path's power did not cure her of whatever ailed her, at least the couple created a colossal memory. Each of us carried an official accordion-style passport that got stamped at cathedrals and hostels to prove in Santiago that we indeed went the distance.

Going the distance on a long trail like the Camino de Santiago includes many instances where we had our perseverance tested. There were some really challenging stretches on the Camino as we crossed several mountain ranges, including the Pyrenees. It was often cold and even snowed at higher elevations.

From ten-year-old, drama-prince-Bryce's journal: *"It was so cold we could see our breath puff in the dark morning air. We had to put plastic bags over our hands to protect them from the chill, and hats under our helmets. Still the wind was so ferociously cold our fingers felt like icy nubs and our legs like bloody stumps. Our cheeks seared in pain as though razors were gouging our skin. Every exposed part of our body was numb and icy while the stinging wind made the feeling of a thousand rusty nails probing our flesh."*

When our family got blasted by high winds on the open plains in the central section, Bryce wrote, *"The wind today was horrid. You had to pedal to go downhill. It was ferocious. It nearly knocked you broadside. We roared in pain and agony. Our legs muscles bulged and tore with exertion. Feeling like broken carcasses, we biked up and down horrible, vast hills and nearly died in the process. The tractor trailers were overpopulated. They roared by, sending us trembling into the briar-seething ditch, and honking their loud horns right in our faces. They also sent a shower of hissing dirt into our eyes. The wave of stinging sand washed over us like a breaking tidal wave and manifested our flesh like a herd of ravenous wasps. I tell you it was plain TORTURE!"*

Bryce was not really suffering on the trip as he did not mention his "agony" when we asked how he was. His answer was always, "I'm fine!" We read our journals out loud to the family every night to share our perspective of the day. I am sure Bryce crafted his words for effect, as he knew he would have an audience to entertain. He liked to dramatize his journal and play with words and probably used humor and tongue-in-cheek exaggeration to help him persevere through the difficult times.

Both children kept up like troopers and never complained. Both children know how to endure uncomfortable situations and possess the self-discipline to accomplish any goal. When you stay out there long enough, you learn that sooner or later the rain stops and the sun comes out, actually and metaphorically. You become stronger. You persevere. The hardship passes.

A self-propelled journey also teaches you that, along the way, there will be an abundance of beauty to grace your days. As on any self-propelled journey, this played a major role in letting us muscle through the hard times. The most stunning section of the Camino was in the westernmost stretch in Galicia. By the time we reached this Celtic-influenced area, we were feeling real strong.

Bryce: *"We soon reached a landscape of what appeared like the Shire from The Lord of the Rings. It was a lumpy road with stone walls covered in emerald moss. The walls had been there for hundreds of years. If you looked over the walls, you could see open fields, seas of grass, rippling with a cool welcoming breeze. The shire road curved lazily over emerald swells where cattle and sheep roamed in flocks. Trees threw shade across the road and streams as clear as rainwater gurgled across it at several places. Today was so beautiful. Now I know what it's like to be a hobbit."*

At journey's end in Santiago, we entered the Cathedral of St James's via the Portico de la Gloria (Port of Glory). In the massive middle column of the doorway is the Tree of Jesse, which depicts Christ's ancestors carved in marble. For centuries, arriving pilgrims have created a ritual by placing their right hand in the middle of the central column. Grooves have been worked in by the tens of thousands of pilgrims as they murmured a prayer of thanks to St. James for their completed journey. We participated in the ancient tradition, placing finger by finger in the indentations, feeling humble like all those who came before us.

At the Pilgrim Mass celebration, a team of eight red-robed monks lit the famous Botafumerio, the largest incense burner in the world, weighing nearly two hundred pounds when filled. They hoisted it on heavy ropes using a system of pulleys that was suspended from the dome. It swung dramatically across the width of the cathedral; back and forth with great precision, spewing a cloud of incense and smoke. Its original function was to clean the air back in the Middle Ages when crowds of dirty, stinky, trail-worn pilgrims filled the church.

The Botafumerio arched like a pendulum, gaining momentum, reaching speeds of forty-two mph in only one-and-a-half minutes. It swung from high in the ceiling to a few feet from the cathedral floor and the heads of the congregation. The dozens of pilgrims and the congregation of eight hundred stood in awe, witnessing the spectacle. Then the organ blasted and the choir sang, while the entire audience exploded in applause. It was so incredibly moving, especially for the pilgrims present. Tears streamed uncontrollably down our cheeks for we realized we had just accomplished a great thing.

An outsider may be tempted to see these self-propelled treks of our family as being physically extreme. Many adults would not entertain the idea of trekking five hundred miles solo, let alone bringing their children along. They see it as simply too much work and don't realize the gifts. Besides our family, there were no other families traveling the length of the Camino. There were *never* any families on any of our long self-propelled adventures, but my intent is to change that with the help of this book.

Understand that this was our family's version of organized sports. Since Sierra and Bryce never stayed home long enough to participate in team sports, we instead chose sports like cycling, hiking, and paddling long distance as a way to compete, only they did so with themselves, and with the entire family. Our "team" was our family. Few think it strange for an athlete to push themselves to exhaustion and nausea when training for a running race or a football game. We just cycled, hiked, and paddled trails instead, but got to do it with our best friends, our family.

We exercised throughout the year doing the same sports that we loved but on a smaller scale. It enabled us to stay fit, so we could more easily tough it out on longer treks. Maintaining fitness became a way of life and enabled us to live a healthier lifestyle. Every member of our family found great pleasure in moving in the great outdoors, despite its accompanying challenges and the need to persevere. It was a very satisfying way to experience the world.

When it came to our level of perseverance, Todd and I have been accused of being "obsessed." We have a need to finish anything that we start. On long trails, people are often tempted to skip around the hard parts, but they also serve an important purpose. They give you a new reference point when you compare "hardship." When someone says it is "windy," your memory will bring you back to that time you tried to cross the open Spanish plain with an incredible headwind on a loaded bike, while tractor trailers blew you off balance. "Windy" will never again mean the same thing to you and the experience will help you deal with the next hardship, because you know you made it through the last. It builds confidence. Every storm you get through makes you that much stronger for whatever is coming down the pike.

My children never entertained the idea of quitting a trail once we began it, no matter how difficult it became, unless something happened beyond our control, like becoming injured, which happened to both Todd and me. We each broke a foot—me on the Appalachian Trail, and Todd on the Pacific Crest Trail. We just returned to finish what we started once we healed or in the next hiking season.

Twenty-five-year-old Bryce said in retrospect: *"In my whole life, on any self-propelled adventure, I never considered quitting as an option. There was never any reason to, or a good enough reason to. If it was shitty sometimes, you just muscled through it. No matter what, you had to keep going. That's how it was always done in my family. If there was a river in the way, you had to figure a way to get across. There were always enough cool, stimulating, interesting things happening to have me not want to quit. If you grow up with parents who don't quit, you, yourself, don't even entertain it as an option in your own life."*

Todd and I raised our children to not be quitters, but to be people who were not afraid to work hard at what they believed in, and persevere until they attained their goal. It wasn't until they were older and more cognizant did they begin to understand what was actually occurring on our family's self-propelled adventures. Before that, it was just a way to live, dreaming big dreams, pursuing far-fetched goals, and never giving it a lot of thought.

ON FOOT

THE PAINE CIRCUIT-TORRES DEL PAINE NATIONAL PARK

It was in Patagonia, South America, where Sierra and Bryce's eyes were opened to who their parents are, how closely we were tied to this trait of perseverance, and who they became because of how they were raised.

Cyclone-force winds raced across the surface of Lake Pehoe in Chile's Torres del Paine National Park, scooping up kiloliters of water and flinging it high in the air in enormous curtains. The sun infused these sky waves with light, creating dazzling rainbows, before they cascaded back to earth. The lake's color was pistachio green, looking more like Thailand than an alpine lake. The gigantic rollers smashed the shoreline mimicking a turbulent ocean, steep enough to surf. We never saw anything like it. But in one of South America's finest national parks, the wind, like the spectacular scenery, was like no other place else on earth.

Patagonia looks like "Alaska on steroids," my kids remarked. It is widely considered more beautiful than the Himalayas, the Alps, New Zealand, the High Sierra, and Alaska. Everything is staggering in beauty and magnitude. Hikers are the only things that feel small in this Patagonian universe.

Our family came over on Sierra's college winter break to backpack the eighty-seven mile Paine Circuit. The trail circles the Paine massif of ten-thousand-foot peaks and climbs alongside a 240-mile long glacier, before ascending to a wind-tunnel pass and looping back around. It is considered one of the top ten best treks in the world.

Patagonia's weather was bizarre, even in the summer. One minute it batters you with frigid cold, spitting hail and driving sleet; fifteen minutes later, you could be dripping in sweat, ripping off rain gear, and slathering on sunscreen—the ozone hole is directly overhead.

Sometimes it rained when the sky was a brilliant blue overhead, for the precipitation was carried from miles away on the wild winds. The weather couldn't make up its mind: it was as if someone was up in the clouds flicking a switch on and off.

Hiking here was challenging, for the trail was often laden with rock rubble and roots. It climbed and descended steeply, like a roller coaster. We crossed rivers on swinging suspension bridges, or by rock-hopping. We often had to wait for the wind to take a breather so that we could cross without getting blown in. Sometimes we had to walk right through the frigid water—water that was locked in an ancient glacier just an hour before. A few ravines had fifty-foot-long steel ladders to assist us.

Conditions in Patagonia were some of the most severe we had ever encountered. We had experienced challenges on other long hikes, but never so many stuffed into one week. We sometimes wondered if it was worth it. We wanted to successfully attain our goal and have fun doing it. After all, we've always told the kids, "It isn't always fun, but it is always worthwhile."

Despite the challenges, Patagonia doesn't disappoint. At the Valle de Frances, we stood atop a ridge surrounded by stunning rock pinnacles. Spires of chiseled stone emerged from the cloud factory, their tops frosted in snow, impossibly sheer, trailing robes of glaciers at their feet. Ice chunks bobbed in the ultramarine lakes, calved off from the glaciers, appearing as if the blue sky itself was contained inside. The turbulent rivers ran milk white from glacial sediment. There were oceans of flowers—hillsides so thick with daisies that from above, it looked like snow covered the ground and walking through them nearly made us seasick from their bobbing, wind-blown heads. Guanacos grazed on the grasslands. Condors, with their ten-foot wing span, glided around the peaks. Patagonia was so stunning and otherworldly that we half expected to see prehistoric beasts walking the valley floors.

Eighteen-year-old Sierra wrote: *"The trail was the most fatiguing hiking I've ever done, dipping up and down, clamoring over rocks all day. I staggered into camp at night, but even so, it was such gorgeous hiking that it was impossible not to be thrilled with happiness. We camped that night on an incredible beach slammed by luminous blue waves that washed icebergs ashore. Carrying our dinner down to a log on the beach, we watched the sun sink behind the Patagonian Mountains. It's days like this I live for. Sometimes I wish I could spend all my time in the mountains, but what good would that do the world?"*

The evening before we climbed over the high pass, we met hikers coming from the opposite direction—young people who looked beaten up and ragged, their chins low, slumped over from exhaustion. They told us stories of how difficult the pass was, trying to give us advice on how long of a day to plan and where to camp (different than our family's plan as we hoped to go further). They glanced at Todd and my gray hair and expressed doubt, as though we were old and incapable of accomplishing what we hoped to do. Sierra and Bryce listened to all of this. Their account raised concern in our minds, but we knew we would just take our time and go slow. I believe in what Confucius taught, "It does not matter how slowly you go as long as you do not stop."

Climbing up alongside the enormous shoulder of Grey Glacier, we thought about the fact that this ice field was the most extensive outside the world's polar regions. The field of ice literally filled the valley and choked the mountain ranges, rearing up like a bowed back of an animal as it swallowed entire rock islands. It was creased with deep blue wrinkles like elephant skin, a color too vivid to be natural. You couldn't see the glacier's source, for it spread for 240 miles, the most massive ice cap south of the Arctic. It was often consumed in blinding light and fog as if it had flowed out of the sky. It was impossible to tell where one let off and the other began.

The wind was ferocious up in the pass. It roared off the glacier and propelled us up and over, inflating our rain gear like we were balloons tethered to the earth by our heavy backpacks. When we yelled with pride at the monument marking the pass, the wind ripped the sound right out of our mouths.

After the pass, Sierra and Bryce looked at Todd and me and said, "You two are bad asses." Todd and I looked at one another and said, "Not really. This is who we are. This is what we have always done."

Up until this point, our children had not invested a lot of time into thinking about who their parents were: two people who have made a life of setting goals and accomplishing them, from big dreams like hiking the Triple Crown, to building a log home from scratch, to smaller ones like cycling the Camino and backpacking the Paine Circuit with our children.

What Sierra and Bryce meant by that comment was that Todd and I possessed a lot of endurance, perseverance, and self-discipline. Up until that "ah-ha" moment, Sierra and Bryce had just been coming along for the ride. When they were younger, they weren't consciously aware of this concept of setting big goals and working to accomplish them. They were following our lead and simply living it, for the lifestyle naturally resonated with them too. At eighteen and twenty, they had a voice in the matter and their eyes finally opened, perhaps also to whom *they* had grown into.

A self-propelled journey gave our family the gift of time and circumstance to discover what we were made of. Bringing our children along on these journeys gifted them with this opportunity too. Can we build on ourselves as if we were slabs of clay, adding chunks as we grow stronger, become bigger people; or, shave off slices of what doesn't fit anymore, as we lose a few pounds of emotional fat?

Life is a test and it challenges us. We went out there to build reserves, add to the coffers, and store up the goods for any hard times ahead. The Pennsylvania mountain man Nessmunk once said, "We don't come out here to rough it. We come out here to smooth it. We get it rough enough at home." So here was this strange, seeming contradiction of circumstances. In roughing it on the trail, persevering through the hard times, life somehow becomes, in the long run, smoother.

Our family's high adventure treks improved personal fitness, taught perseverance and self-reliance, and built a knowledge of the outdoors.

The legendary Boy Scouts Fifty Miler Award is close to what our family sets out to do, including an understanding of conservation. Their goal is to cover the trail or canoe/kayak route of not less than fifty miles, without the aid of motors, and take a minimum of five consecutive days to complete the trip. Along the way, they must give back and perform ten service hours on projects to improve the trail, springs, campsite, portage, or area. Getting your child involved in the scouting program is a good way to introduce them to a self-propelled journey if you cannot lead or participate yourself.

BY BOAT

PADDLING THE WILDERNESS TRAIL,
EVERGLADES NATIONAL PARK

The Everglades National Park is called "the last great wilderness experience in Florida." That statement alone lured me in, for I knew a self-propelled paddling journey executed in this national park would have much to teach our family. Over winter break in 2011, I asked our young adult children if they wanted to travel to the Everglades for a little adventure.

"Yes," Sierra said, "but we must do something epic, not just drive around sight-seeing." If our children were going to gift us with their presence, adventure had to be a component. The Everglades are a watery world. "How could you possibly do it right in a vehicle?" the kids asked. The goal of travel is to become connected to a place and have it become part of you, so we chose paddling the hundred-mile-long Wilderness Trail from the top of the Everglades National Park to the bottom.

We loaded two canoes with supplies and enough food and water for ten days. We traversed bays, narrow streams loaded with alligators, and mangrove swamps while camping on islands or on elevated wooden "chickies" surrounded by water.

The challenges were many. The Everglades are nicknamed "River of Grass," but on this water trail, not a blade of grass could be found.

Navigating a water trail was very tricky and needed some getting used to. We mounted a boat compass on the rental canoe and I had another around my neck. I constantly studied the map. I used a pair of binoculars to search for the channel markers, which were often obscure. We used a weather radio so weather fronts coming through bringing vicious waves and relentless winds would not surprise us and we could prepare.

We learned about *fetch*—the area/amount of open water the wind has to blow across until it reaches you. It builds and gathers velocity the longer the expanse. We needed to bear this in mind when crossing large expanses of open water with wind. We had to plan which angle to paddle in, tacking like a sailboat, to prevent rollers from capsizing us and to use them to help propel us forward.

The sun was relentless at times for there was virtually no shade. We wore very thin, long-sleeved shirts, brimmed hats, sunglasses, and we lathered on plenty of sunscreen. There were also four days when we did not touch solid ground. In that stretch, we slept on chickies in the middle of a body of water. Except for the port-a-potties at these campsites, the only way to relieve ourselves in this stretch was by hanging our butt overboard. When camping on islands, we could not have gallon jugs of water in plain view, for raccoons (who are thirsty too) puncture each and every container.

Out of everything, Todd was most concerned that one of our boats would be overturned. With all our weight and gear, and with virtually no land in sight, capsizing would make it extremely challenging to recover our gear, bail out the water, and reboard. To minimize the risk of getting caught in dangerous weather, we rose early in the morning when skies were the calmest and covered a chunk of some miles before the wind built up.

The adventures were many. After ten days, the whole paddle seemed to blend and melt into one wonderfully watery experience. It was the actual living on the water for that extended period of time that became so special, especially the four days in a row where we slept on chickies and never touched terra firma. I was afraid we would become bored as we all liked to move more than sit in camp. We're strong paddlers and our assigned schedule (from the National Park Service) included some very short days. However, disconnecting from technology and society (there is little cell service in some areas), as well as seeing only a handful of boats the entire time, proved to be rejuvenating.

We paddled about two miles per hour so there was time to sing, make plans, share dreams, and check in with our kids. Sometimes, we just dipped our paddles quietly, and seemed to dissolve into the timeless waters of the Everglades. Paddling slowed down our fast-paced, action-packed lives.

The wildlife was captivating. Schools of dolphins raced alongside our canoes and played underneath. Dozens of alligators sunned themselves only a mere few feet away as we snuck through the infamous "Nightmare" passage and narrow, winding Gopher Creek. We came upon vulture rookeries with fifty of the magnificent birds studding the tree tops like angels on Christmas trees. There were so many birds, the trees and bushes were white-washed from their droppings. If it was cool out, they perched with their great wings spread out, soaking up the heat with their dark feathers. There were swimming manatees, rare sawfish in the waters, white ibises, and herons to watch.

Alligators actually snored through the night. Occasionally we'd hear a slap as we lay in our tents and knew that a fish's life had just ended. The circle of life was taking place all around us. At night, the number of stars was breathtaking and when they reflected back into the water surrounding our chickie, they seemed to double. In camp, we played cards, wrote in our journals, read good books, and sipped tea. It was a luxury to spend such an extended period of time together with absolutely no outside distractions. The best part of the Wilderness Trail was being together as a family.

Todd had been nervous about casting off for ten days into the wilderness with our heavily loaded canoes. This whole idea of leaving the safety of the shore behind felt like a metaphor for Sierra and Bryce's life with their parents, their guides throughout their childhood, as they would soon be cast into adulthood. On all the other long paddling trips, Todd and I each had a child in the bow of our boat. On this trip, Sierra and Bryce powered their own together, separate from Todd's and mine.

I listened to my children's singing across the bay, their sweet voices and happy laughter carrying over the water. They stroked in unison. I felt great joy in knowing that they seemed equipped to go out there in life on their own. They had the necessary tools, they had each other. That will always remain the case, long after Todd and I are gone. That is what we hoped to nurture and build, beginning with those very first years on the Continental Divide Trail; to trust, not just their parents, but in themselves, each other, and the big world.

On our self-propelled Everglades adventure, this virtue of perseverance was called upon in a different context compared to our other adventures. We were not challenged to overcome actual hardship created by adverse conditions, but it was more about overcoming fears and navigating through the muddy waters of doubt. Sierra and Bryce witnessed their father struggling with his concerns—wind, capsizing, route finding, etc.—and how that could have ruined our family's good time. Both Todd and I felt as if we were ultimately in charge of keeping our children safe, regardless of their age, but Todd especially has always embraced and adopted his role as Trail Boss. It took some days on the water for Todd to gain the confidence and the experience to believe that he and his family could do this trip, be safe, learn a lot, and have a great time. In observing their father persevere through his self-doubts, they too learned how to believe in themselves and their skills.

After this epic paddle, we expected to know the Everglades a little more intimately. This is always one of the goals of travel, to become connected to a place and have it become part of us. An added bonus was to learn a little more about ourselves along the way.

Our adventure in the Everglades reminded me of a quote I have always loved from a small book called *On the Loose*, by Jerry and Terry Russell. They wrote,

"One of the best-paying professions is getting ahold of pieces of country in your mind, learning their smell and their moods, sorting out the pieces of a view, deciding what grows there and why, how many steps that hill will take, where this creek winds and where it meets the other one below. . . . This is the best kind of ownership, and the most permanent."

While Sierra and Bryce have learned how to persevere through self-propelled travel, they more importantly have become courageous, hard-working adults along the way. These self-propelled travels provided some of the best theaters for conducting this learning.

NUTS AND BOLTS

A family cannot just hop onto a long-distance, self-propelled journey without substantial prior experience. Part of our responsibility as parents is to lead our children safely through the world, and in our family, that includes the wilderness! Parents will have to build up to longer distance but it is certainly attainable. Once your family identifies the sport they enjoy the most, and once you have acquired the necessary gear to participate, start small. Build slowly, from an overnighter, to a long weekend, to a weeklong vacation. Join hiking, canoeing, and cycling clubs to gain experience and glean knowledge from seasoned outdoorspeople. Besides regional clubs, also check out organizations such as the Sierra Club outings and the Appalachian Mountain Club. I joined our local Blue Mountain Eagle Climbing Club based in Reading, Pennsylvania, when I was only fifteen years old and learned much from the club's elders on those early trips. And of course, the scouting program provides wonderful opportunities, especially the teenage program, Venture Crew, which includes girls on high adventure trips. A parent can also get involved as a leader and as a result, all learn the sport together.

Look for organized journeys to participate in. For example, Pennsylvania has a wonderful program called River Sojourns, which sponsors long river trips under the Pennsylvania Organization for Watersheds and Rivers, Inc. These guided paddling trips range from two to nine days and include meals, transfers, and camping for the reasonable cost of $20–$75 a day. Trained safety personnel accompany the sojourns and many have rental boats available through local liveries. Over a dozen opportunities exist in any calendar year and participants are not limited to those living within the state. You do not have to be a Pennsylvanian in order to participate.

Another way to gain experience is for parents to enroll in instruction courses, often put on by the local clubs, or the American Canoe Association. Parents should be up to date on their First Aid regardless of the sport they participate in. Check out the Red Cross for ongoing first aid courses.

BIKE RIDING IN STEPS

The Camino was not our family's first self-propelled cycling adventure. Starting with 650 miles along New Mexcio's Great Divide Mountain Bike Trail, when the kids were six and eight years old, the children first viewed the world from the back of a tandem. For four years, it was a brilliant way to show young children the world. But before long, a child will ache for the freedom of powering their own bike, and rightfully so. It is an important step in developing their independence.

After our family's six-week cycling tour of Ireland in 2001, ten- and twelve-year-old Sierra and Bryce announced that they had had enough of staring at Mom and Dad's backs. They wanted to power their own bikes. Cycling the Camino was on our radar as an upcoming trip but we warned the kids that it would be tough. The route included crossing the mountainous Pyrenees as well the windy interior. Todd and I told them that they'd have to carry their own gear in bike panniers and haul themselves up and down mountains using their own leg power. They were ready, they insisted. To test if this was so, we made a three-week cycling trip to the flat Yucatan Peninsula before they tackled the more challenging, hilly Camino. In this way, our family learned and experienced self-propelled travel in steps.

CHAPTER 10

Learning from Pushing past Your Comfort Zone

The Old Man of the Earth stooped over the floor of the cave, raised a huge stone from it, and left it leaning. It disclosed a great hole that went plumb-down.
"That is the way," he said.
"But there are no stairs."
"You must throw yourself in. There is no other way."
George MacDonald, *The Golden Key*

ON MOUNTAINS

From a distance, Mount Katahdin's Knife Edge in northern Maine looked like a fin on a dinosaur's back, the work of two glaciers that gouged the sides off this ridge. The slope dropped two thousand feet on either side of a mile-long "trail," which was sometimes no wider than our bodies. On those spots, we could not walk upright. Instead, we pulled ourselves along, bellies hugging the rock. The further along the ridge we inched, the more technically difficult the hike became. We had to help each other over spots, looking for hand and footholds.

Our family and friends were climbing "the greatest mountain" in Baxter State Park, the northern terminus of the National Scenic Appalachian Trail (AT). The AT is the longest continuously marked footpath in the world and our group was commemorating the twentieth anniversary of my long thru-hike, which I completed in 1979. Instead of returning via the AT, we chose the more scenic, yet precipitous, Knife Edge to create a loop. To celebrate afterwards, we overnighted in a cabin at Chimney Pond.

Sierra and Bryce were pumped for the crossing. They were seven and nine years old at the time and had just recently hiked the last 250 miles of the Continental Divide Trail in Colorado and cycled 650 miles of New Mexico on the Great Divide Mountain Bike Trail. They were strong and in shape, regardless of their young age, and when it came to rock scrambling, they were in their element.

The drop-offs were all fogged in. There wasn't a hint of the ridge's extreme exposure. A few of the adults along were not very experienced or as fit as our family and were quite fearful. My girlfriend, Beth Ellen, gripped Sierra's raincoat sleeve with such force and frequency that she ripped it right off. Our family had to take care of the other adults, wait for them, and encourage them. Then it began to rain lightly and the adults grew even more concerned.

Once you are halfway across the Knife Edge, there is no choice but to continue, push through, and hope you can get to safety, if and when conditions deteriorate. Todd and I did not think that Sierra and Bryce were weaker than the adults along when it came to enduring hardship. They might have even been stronger. They had many wilderness adventures and had been in situations that demanded far more from them than the Knife Edge. They knew how to rise to the challenge. They understood the need to pace yourself and knew that difficult stretches did not last forever.

Climbing mountains teaches courage. Courage is the ability to do something that frightens you. It is not the absence of fear but the ability to conquer it that enables a person to face difficulty, danger, and even pain. Courage has the capacity to inform and strengthen others. It makes all the other virtues possible. Todd and I believed that much could be learned from climbing mountains and so we brought Sierra and Bryce onto their backbones as often as we could.

On the Knife Edge, I continually checked in with Sierra and Bryce, asking if they were okay. Not only did they pull their bodies over the rocks with balance and grace, they never ran out of energy or lost a sense of joy. They sang. They were having the time of their lives.

When we reached Chimney Pond and our cabin for the night, the adults collapsed on the chairs, while our kids asked if they could *go outside to play*. The twelve-mile day had not fazed them. Certainly, the emotional drama of the Knife Edge that some of the adults endured had not exhausted them either. As the day drew to a close, the kids burst through the cabin door, faces glowing, and exclaimed, "This has been the best day, Mom!"

The account of our hike appeared as the cover story of *The Appalachian Trailway News*, the official periodical of the Appalachian Trail Conservancy. In the following issue, to my surprise, multiple letters to the editor appeared, referencing our cover story. They were written by senior hikers chastising us for what they thought to be irresponsible parenting. They thought we had no business being out there with children, in inclement weather. "We were fine," the kids said, when I read them the letters. "The other adults were freaking out. They had the hard time, not us."

If you push yourself out of your comfort zone, the situation can *appear* risky. The seniors who wrote letters to the editor felt pushed past their own comfort zone as they read the story, even though our children were not out of their element.

We responded to the editor with information about who these cover children were, what they had accomplished in their short lives, and that we were very experienced long-distance backpackers. We'd logged over ten thousand miles at that point, and a good chunk of that was with our kids in tow.

Baxter State Park officials have rules pertaining to when they feel it is safe to climb Mount Katahdin. Our anniversary day had not been a forbidden climb; it just had an advisory warning attached to it. Todd and I heeded that advice and proceeded with caution, wisdom, and experience. We also had a sleeping bag and stove for emergency purposes. Todd and I were no strangers to wilderness travel, were good at sizing up potential risks, and prided ourselves on making good judgment calls that have led to a safe, yet adventurous, life for our children.

Our children were not scared on the Knife Edge because they had years of examples where their parents performed as very good leaders. We were good at assessing risk and would not behave foolhardily, dangerously, or stupidly. Our children were used to working as a team; they knew how to take directions and follow instructions. Sierra and Bryce did not have to muster up any courage to traverse the Knife Edge, unlike the adults in their company, neither physical nor moral courage. They had full confidence in their parents and that gave them confidence in themselves. They would follow us across the Knife Edge and almost anywhere we led them.

Every day, parents try to balance on the same knife edge of life, making decisions about what is right or wrong, safe or dangerous, too indulgent or too challenging for their young children. Some parents think they need to protect their children from everything, that there are dangers lurking everywhere. It is a fact of life that all movement entails some risk. But if you do not play and you are not psychically active, there is even greater risk. It just takes longer to manifest itself, in sickness and disease later in life. Overprotective or helicopter parents are not giving their children many opportunities to test their courage nor challenge their ability to cope.

Throughout our lives, Todd and I have enjoyed pushing ourselves beyond our comfort zones. We reveled in the elevated excitement that accompanied it, and how it made us feel alive. More importantly, these accomplishments fostered confidence and strength. The character-building and life skills that were acquired while executing activities like traversing Knife Edge ridges gave us the courage to navigate across other challenges that would inevitably come up in life.

Before we even became parents, it was understood that we would raise our children in the same vein as we continued having exciting adventures. I gathered mental notes about raising kids long before we arrived in those years, in hopes of being better prepared. Sometimes, that information came from unusual sources, like in art school. When I was an art student, I had a part-time job as an artist's model and continued working at a local university for a few years after I became a parent. Partially for income, partially to stay connected to youth in hopes of being a more understanding parent, my contact with these young adults taught me a lot. I often conversed with them from the modeling stand.

From my perch, I saw that one young woman had so many tattoos and piercings on her face that it was difficult to tell what her features truly looked like. I understood tattooing is a popular body modification in today's culture and many use their skin as a canvas to display art, but this seemed excessive. A dog collar with lethal-looking spikes encircled her neck. Down her bosom draped chains that were beefy enough to pull a jeep out of the mud and one had a large combination lock hanging from it as a "fashion pendant." She wasn't the only student before me that had piercings but she was the most decorated. She smiled at me when she caught me looking at her and her countenance was sweet.

"Can anyone tell me why they get pierced?" I asked the room of students.

"It is an adrenalin rush when the needle goes in," the girl with the dog collar explained. "It makes me feel alive. And it makes me crave that feeling, so I keep getting more piercings so I can keep experiencing it."

Wow, I thought. I could relate to the love of adrenalin, the need for excitement and pushing the envelope. Many young people are predisposed to taking risks and it is part of their natural development. If a young person does not discover healthy outlets for adrenalin rushes and testing, they could possibly experiment with drugs, drinking, speeding cars, gambling. Sitting on that modeling stand, I thought about how incredibly challenging it is to navigate through these years. Parents need to have as many tools in their tool box as possible to help our children come out the other side unscathed.

Todd and I wanted to model a way of life for Sierra and Bryce where they could learn to stretch themselves and seek endless possibilities. We wanted to show them how to create a life that is full of new ideas, skills, opportunities and experiences, a life where you make things happen rather than waiting for them to happen *to you*. If you see your comfort zone as a series of concentric circles, you won't expand as a human being unless you push beyond the circle of comfort you are in. Everyone is at a different level. Everyone has a good idea where their own personal comfort zone ends. The idea is to challenge yourself but not put yourself in danger; stop before you physically and emotionally fall apart.

We found many opportunities to push past our comfort zones and used them to develop certain values like courage in our children, at home and abroad, in the city and in the wilds. Although there are many different arenas in which to teach your children the associated lessons, our favorite way was in the natural world, scaling mountains, paddling rivers, hiking trails, and climbing peaks. Half Dome in Yosemite National Park was our all-time most spectacular—and most challenging—climb.

In our Half Dome adventure, we wavered back and forth when it came to our decision making. Because of changing conditions, we were forced to assess and reassess the risk. Just because you make one decision on a climb or a decision in life in general, it does not mean you can't change your mind part way through. One is not wedded to a decision, but can modify or change it in response to experience or new information.

HALF DOME HIKE

The 8,800-foot granite dome is Yosemite National Park's icon, the symbol of what some consider America's most beautiful national park. It rises five thousand abrupt feet from the valley floor and besides being a popular technical rock climbing route up its sheer face, it is also a very popular hiking route. The Half Dome hike is considered a "walk up," where you do not need technical experience, but it still takes a lot of work to just get to its base. A fifteen-mile hike up from the valley floor with an altitude accumulation of 3,800 feet is necessary to reach it. The last 400 feet to the summit have upright cables for your hands and wooden posts for resting. They enable hikers to scale the remaining pitch of this granite national natural landmark without rock climbing equipment.

Todd and I hiked Half Dome twice before, back when you could sleep atop this amazing dome. The weather had been clear and calm and it was one of the most memorable nights I have ever spent on this planet. The view of Yosemite Valley is perhaps the most stunning in America and what you must go through to attain it—the climb up the exposed cables—is completely unique. When Bryce was seventeen years old, we brought him to California to share this unforgettable place. Living on the East Coast, we do not have many opportunities to hike an unusual granite monolith like Half Dome. It is what we came to Yosemite to do and so we were going to accept the challenge if it was at all possible. The deteriorating weather we were experiencing, however, was making our decision to climb a tough one.

Bryce: *"When we reached the base of Half Dome, mist was rolling in and it started to drizzle. Cables spanned its nearly vertical face, interspersed with metal posts and loose wooden slats. It was more than a little intimidating and the few hikers descending were putting on a show. One guy was hooking himself into the metal cables with a carabineer at every metal post. A few hikers were sliding so terribly down the wet rock that they slammed their groins into the wood slats to stop."*

We watched the sliding hikers, holding our breath, hoping that they would stay safe. When the hikers finally got down, they said they had very little traction and that their arms were very sore. They appeared to be very shook up. Todd and I told Bryce, no, we would not climb. It was not worth the risk. It was a good reason to return someday.

Some hikers find that the Half Dome hike pushes them to their limit—the feeling of exposure is that intense. Accidents off the cables, however, are extremely rare. Thousands hike it every year and there have been only a handful of deaths during the summer. Since 1919, only three have died when the cables were up for summer use.

But then the sun came out and a group of foreigners arrived at the base of the cables and began to climb. They were not slipping. We studied the sky and tried to decide if the weather was improving. Great clouds of fog blew in and engulfed the dome. Teasing little slits of blue sky appeared.

The sun began staying out longer. The sky was bluer. Views were opening up and it appeared to be rapidly drying the granite. We reconsidered our decision. Todd and I wanted to be responsible parents, while giving Bryce the freedom to help make the final decision.

"Let's do it," we all finally decided.

Bryce wrote: *"The rock wasn't overly slick, but the exposure was enough to make your mind reel. All I could do was grip on for dear life and mutter words of amazement. Relying on the loose cables and my Gollum-style climbing skills, I managed to summit the peak, followed by surprisingly unshaken parents."*

Before we reached the summit, the rain resumed. Clouds moved in with no visible break. If it rained for hours, we could be stranded on the summit, soaked, risking hypothermia. It could get so much worse. We took a rapid look around and I announced, "We've got to get down, now!" It rained nearly all the way down but the sun was also out the entire time.

Todd advised Bryce and me to always maintain a strong grip on the cables. If our feet went out from under us, we would stay on the mountain. We slid our hands down the cables, lowering ourselves, foot by foot, stepping very lightly, usually sideways, to gain more surface traction. At one point, my leg vibrated up and down with uncontrollable nerves and fatigue, like a sewing machine needle. Todd later shared that he feared I had pushed myself too far, but the granite dome quickly grew less steep and I regained my strength.

On Half Dome, we teetered on the knife edge between dangerous and safe. Here was a situation where we had trouble calculating risk and safety accurately and could have gotten ourselves into trouble.

Experiences like crossing Katahdin's Knife Edge, summiting Half Dome, and especially navigating the entire 3,100-mile Continental Divide Trail, taught Sierra and Bryce some of their most important lessons about pushing boundaries. Wild, unpredictable nature helped us realize our limits as humans. When you expose yourself to the elements, you learn how vulnerable human life is, how knife-edge easy it is to not survive. You can get hypothermia on a day hike. Some do die out there.

Because of our love of the outdoors, Todd and I chose it as the arena in which we would teach our children the important lessons of pushing boundaries and assessing risk. Most parents will not choose to lead their children in our footsteps. Learning to navigate challenging situations can be experienced on a much smaller scale and in an infinite number of ways and situations, and still teach children the same important lessons. A family can climb a local peak and experience the same feelings of accomplishment; it does not need to be in a remote area nor the activity strenuous. Any time you are recreating outdoors, you may encounter inclement weather. You may need to decide how much water to drink to stay hydrated; when to put on warm clothing so hypothermia does not attack; when to relax in the shade if it's hot to prevent heat stroke. You could be out for a short hike or a bike ride on a rail trail, or in a rental canoe on a lake, or skating on a pond, and important decisions about the weather and your safety may need to be made.

Pushing beyond your comfort zone can teach children lessons that are useful throughout their lives. These lessons provide a map in which to navigate decision making, and craft a way of living that is rich, colorful, and exciting. Parents have to be willing to stick their own necks out, remove themselves from their comfort zone, be willing to push themselves alongside their children, and not preach only limits and boundaries. Children will learn to make choices in their lives that are not based on and controlled by fear.

WITH WILD ANIMALS

GRIZZLY BEARS

When Todd and I first decided to take three-year-old Bryce and five-year-old Sierra llama packing in Montana's Glacier National Park, we knew there were more grizzly bears there than in any other area in the lower forty-eight states. The potential dangers of encountering them needed to be weighed. We did not want to push our family beyond the circle of safety.

Fortunately, the rules for safety are strict in this wild arena; out here, you are not at the top of the food chain. Todd and I contacted wildlife specialists on the proper way to conduct ourselves in the bears' home and how to avoid confrontation. We learned that llamas keep the grizzly at a distance; they respect each other's space, and that there has never been a single encounter between grizzlies and stock in the park's history. We read and educated ourselves on the bears' habits, how to avoid them, and what to do if we encountered one.

In Glacier, Sierra and Bryce never hiked ahead nor were they allowed to fall behind. They were always sandwiched in between adults. When hiking through overgrown areas where the bushes were over our heads, we had to part them and separate them with our hands before going through, never knowing if we would surprise a bear. The kids sang long, repetitive songs like "The Ants Go Marching One by One," and had fun jingling bells to alert the bears of our presence.

Pack llamas normally relax on breaks: sit down, eat, and chew their cud. But for the one hundred miles we hiked through Glacier, our llamas were torqued. They stood at constant attention. They never relaxed. They smelled grizzlies everywhere and the bears were indeed out there.

Hikers without livestock were encountering them left and right. The campsites were closing around us because of their disturbance.

We saw physical signs of their presence everywhere. Rocks and huge boulders were rolled over as they looked for grubs to eat. One area looked like a bulldozer had gone through, the ground torn up from the bears digging for glacial lily tubers. There were scat piles laden with berries so whole and perfect that Bryce said, "I can pick them out and eat them!"

Most parents probably view our Glacier National Park hike as not only crossing the boundaries of comfort but having entered into the high-risk zone. In all the months and all the miles on the Continental Divide Trail, our children never so much as suffered a cold or unwrapped a Band-Aid, and they certainly did not get eaten by a grizzly.

Many people are fearful of bear country so why would the typical parent even consider pushing the envelope by bringing their kids into the wilderness where the Great Bear roams? Grizzlies are found in spectacularly beautiful country, for the creature needs wide expanses that are wild and vacant of man. Once the land is gone, it is gone. It cannot be replaced. Once the grizzly is gone, it can't be brought back either.

Doug Peacock, author of *In the Presence of Grizzlies*, said, "The most important ingredient to carry into grizzly country is your state of mind." This heightened awareness cranked all of our senses up a few notches, as if we had received electric shocks, and we felt more alive than ever before. Even when the kids were small, they were totally absorbed and loved the excitement. We were paying large attention; we were right there in the moment. We were not distracted by politics or cell phones or body image. We were looking at life straight in the eye. There are not many places you can travel to that demand that kind of focus.

There are only a handful of wild animals in North America that are higher on the food chain than man: grizzlies, cougars, and alligators/crocodiles. Crocs only live in the far southern tip of Florida and are few and far between. They are also secretive and very shy. Alligators, on the other hand, are everywhere, and although humans are not typically in their diet, they do pose a marginal threat and one does need to be knowledgeable and cautious when traveling in their home.

ALLIGATORS

OKEFENOKEE SWAMP

When you paddle southern Georgia's Okefenokee National Wildlife Refuge, your constant companion is the alligator, for more than thirteen thousand make their home in the tea-colored waters of America's largest swamp. When the kids were ten and twelve years old, we took them on a five-day paddling trip over Thanksgiving holiday. Besides the alligators, we also went for the cypress forests cloaked in eerie Spanish moss, the brilliant lilies in watery prairies, and the frogs, turtles, and abundant bird life. We paddled our way to remote wooden chickies, where we slept amongst the wild swamp creatures. The Okefenokee is a fine place for children, for it is fiercely entertaining. If you keep a respectable distance, the alligators add an element of excitement.

We spent most of the five days looking for alligators and got really good at it. It was a constant game of "I Spy." We scoped the shores for them as they lazily sunned themselves on the grassy banks. We found them in the shallows beneath the overhanging bushes and trees. Sometimes we saw nests of dozens of babies. In the water, we looked for grey/black logs with bumps. Usually, we only saw the tops of their heads sticking out of the black water, gliding silently, like moving logs with eyeballs. They floated across the water so slowly and then sank like a heavy log and disappeared. We wondered how many were under us that we didn't even see. Some absolutely did not want to move and so we got up close and personal with them. One day we spotted more than sixty.

When we arrived at one particular camp, the wooden sleeping platform had a big bull alligator sunning on it. He looked like he owned the place. Our approaching canoes forced him to slide into the dark water and we forgot about him, until right before we went to sleep. A gurgling, bubbling sound was coming from the water a few inches away on the other side of the thin, nylon tent wall. The creature hunted and splashed through the night, keeping us awake. Sierra slept on that end of the tent, so she drew close and cuddled, worried it would come and get her in the night. Its movements and close proximity *sounded* dangerous, but knowing its behavior and habits, we felt the risk extremely low. We were safe in our tent.

One day in the swamp, we spied one of the largest alligators we ever saw, maybe fourteen feet long, sunning himself in a narrow channel. I wanted a better look for a photo so Bryce and I paddled closer. I assumed the alligator would head in the opposite direction up the channel if he felt threatened. But he took his powerful forearms, which looked like he lifted weights (he did, his own body!) and scrambled towards us! We were in the way of his escape route. I yelled, "Paddle backwards!" to Bryce. We laughed afterwards but my drama boy said he would remain "scarred for the rest of his life." This encounter did give us a renewed respect for this wild, potentially dangerous creature.

Should parents avoid places where potentially dangerous wild animals roam? Should children miss out on experiencing the majesty of places like Glacier National Park and the Okefenokee Swamp? The trips to these wild places rank as some of our best memories and all-time favorite trips, although educating ourselves on the animals' habits and exercising caution was necessary. Being in the beautiful home of these wild animals humbled us. There was some risk and danger present, factors we could not control, but these are always present on some level in life. You are far more likely to die in a car accident than get eaten by a wild animal.

Climate change is the result of humankind seeing the natural world as outside of itself, as controllable and exploitable. The planet has its boundaries and we have pushed beyond them. We are now facing the consequences of our flawed belief system. We must learn to change our habits and our relationship with nature. An added value when you spend time outdoors is you come to appreciate the natural world. When you love something, you will work to conserve it, whether it is wild, open space or the river that runs through your town.

What our family has experienced out there, scaling peaks and rubbing shoulders with predators, may appear extreme to most families. Just doing small excursions and activities in the outdoors that are more accessible, will teach the same lessons, cultivate courage, and not involve high risk which parents may not be qualified to lead their children through. For example, you could take children whitewater rafting, but sign up to go with an optional guide in a paddle-assist raft, and don't captain the boat yourself if you don't possess the skills. Backpacking on a scout trip can teach important lessons and provide excellent skilled leadership while learning to push and test a young person's limits.

Todd and I felt that pushing our children's comfort zones in the wilds would better prepare them for whatever lies ahead in their adult lives, which are full of metaphorical "alligators and grizzlies." How do we parents protect them in the "swamp" of life? As the world changes, our children will need more tools to face whatever lies ahead. They are going to inhabit a world that we are not even going to see. There is rapid change, in economics, politics, and climate. One of our jobs as parents is to help our children become more confident and comfortable when dealing with unknowns and having the confidence that they will be able to figure out how to successfully navigate their world without us.

Learning to push beyond your comfort zone gets you in shape for the really important questions and intersections that look risky in your adult life—a job change, a move, a relationship ending or beginning, having a child.

If we purposely work to stay safe in our everyday life, and don't stretch ourselves, we may be incapable of stretching when we're forced to. Decisions will be viewed as overwhelmingly stressful, not joyous and exciting. We won't have enough experience with this type of challenge to know that things often work out and different is not bad. We make our lives what they are, mostly from our attitudes. We cannot insulate our children from tragedy. Accidents, even sickness and death—these are a very real part of life which must be dealt with. But a "safe" comfortable life could lead to a life that is dull, flat, and boring. Do we want a shut-down life, or a life open to infinite possibilities, a big life? We can become used to saying no to life instead of yes, simply because of the unknown.

Todd and I have balanced one another throughout our twenty-plus years of parenting. We did not try to protect Sierra and Bryce from everything, nor did we believe that there were dangers lurking everywhere. Dating back to when they were one and three-year-olds on the Continental Divide, we believed our children were competent and capable for their ages and developmental levels, especially when armed with the right tools, education, and guidance. No creative act or discovery was ever made by doing things exactly the same way it had always been done, without risking or pushing the boundaries. You need to be willing to take on some risks to make discoveries possible. What society originally viewed as crazy ideas, like explorations, experiments, and inventions, can revolutionize and heal the world.

Many parents are afraid to let their children walk to school, climb a tree, take a public bus, let alone scale the Knife Edge or climb Half Dome. Our local state university does not even allow college students to cross a street without a crossing guard. Fear has become the norm. We are doing our children—and the world—a huge disservice by not allowing them to experience risk.

If you forbid a child from doing risky things, you disable and distrust that child's ability to learn. Kids who are raised to not be afraid of risk will develop confidence in their ability to negotiate life, and enjoy life-changing rewards in the end.

Part of what Sierra and Bryce learned about pushing boundaries will need to be applied to their adult lives. Because they were raised alternatively, they risk going against the grain of society, stepping out of the flow and swimming in their own stream, even swimming upstream as they follow their own path. It could be their occupation or lifestyle choice or how they raise their own children or choosing to not live a consuming life. They must learn to follow their own heart, when it looks completely different than what everyone else is doing. Moral courage, not physical, will be needed to forge their own path. Hopefully, the Knife Edge and Half Dome, the grizzly bears and the alligators will have helped them arrive at that place of confidence and belief in themselves.

NUTS AND BOLTS

Much of how children see life and embrace risk depends on how their parents view it. If you live in a scared state of being, seeking comfort and unchanging situations, your children will be influenced by your fear and limits. Part of the joy of bringing children into the world is that they stretch us, force us out of our comfort zone and into varying activities and interests that we never would have considered exploring. Gather as much knowledge as possible and stay as safe as you can, but cast off the mooring lines and explore life with them. If we allow them to, our children can show us how to return to a time where fun and excitement and unbridled joy were the norm. As we grow older, we forget.

CHAPTER 11

Learning to Blaze Your Own Trail

"The stories people tell have a way of taking care of them. If stories come to you, care for them. And learn to give them away where they are needed. Sometimes a person needs a story more than food to stay alive."

Barry Lopez, *Crow and Weasel*

Tell me, I forget
Show me, I remember
Involve me, and I understand

Anonymous

FINDING A PURPOSE IN LEADERSHIP

When fifteen-year-old Sierra attended Schuylkill County's Norm Thornberg Conservation Camp, she felt like an outcast. She wasn't into shooting black powder rifles like most of the kids, for the powerful recoil scared her. She also felt shy in the large group. She did, however, love the knowledge she was fed in the five-day camp, documenting everything in her journal.

Because Sierra wanted to remember everything that she was learning, she was often busy writing in her journal. She cared deeply and personally about every fish, invertebrate, and fern that she discovered. She was the only camper who recorded anything and the other campers thought her a bit strange. But because of her recording, the knowledge stuck. When the leaders surprised the campers with a pop review test, Sierra received the highest grade. No one knew that the winner would receive a full scholarship to attend the two-week Pennsylvania Conservation Camp at University Park the following summer.

The ultimate goal of these nationwide camps is to introduce students to conservation and environmental careers, and to encourage them to pursue these interests. They might learn how to track wildlife, identify native plants, or tie a fly. From stream sampling of fish and aquatic life, to forestry skills, daily activities are planned to get students out in the field to meet and observe environmental professionals. The camps are usually targeted to teens age fourteen to eighteen. Professionals in the field teach many of the hands-on classes and learning is the kind that lasts: experiential learning. When students leave these camps, they have a keen awareness of the outdoor world and the many careers found there. They also have the desire to become tomorrow's stewards of the natural world.

Sierra wasn't just acquiring information at these camps, she was becoming self-knowledgeable. She was learning what her personal characteristics, abilities, motives, and feelings were. Out of all the values and traits and banks of knowledge Sierra and Bryce received over their childhood, this kind of knowledge—who they are—is perhaps the most important. With greater self-knowledge, you are able to understand how your thoughts and feelings came about and how they influence your behavior. Armed with this knowledge, you can make life happen *for* you rather than *to* you.

After our county's local camp, Sierra attended our state-level conservation camp, Pennsylvania's Conservation Leadership School. She learned how to manage sustainable forests, care for wildlife, analyze her hometown drinking water, balance deer population, recycle, and do green construction.

Sierra went on to attend the Schuylkill River Outreach Team that same summer, a camp where teens traveled throughout the county, learning about the Schuylkill River Watershed. This small group of eight lived out of a van and visited mine reclamation sites, riparian zones, and dumps, while looking at land conservation issues. They constructed wildlife platforms to provide homes for waterfowl, observed acid mine drainage, toured water filtering facilities, and went on float trips to haul tires out of the river. At the same time, they were learning what a powerful effect a group of like-minded individuals can have on one another. If they bonded as friends, it didn't matter if they were cleaning up a disgusting dump; they could still have fun and make a positive difference. Only a few experiences in a young person's life impact them to the point where they are propelled down a particular path and are forever changed. These conservation camps did that for Sierra.

Sierra was moved to create a more permanent, frequent gathering of young conservationists. With the help of her river outreach advisor, Tom Davidock, Sierra formed the Schuylkill County Conservation Club, pooling students from the local public schools. In a two-year period, the club conducted more than twenty conservation projects, which Sierra orchestrated. It became about educating others: students, participants, and her whole community. It also gave Sierra the opportunity to come into her own and blossom.

At this time, Sierra had just left public school and had begun to orchestrate her own learning. Only a few years had passed since she was in middle school, when she was challenged by her girlfriends. They had become jealous of her freedom to come and go as she pleased. My children were missing an average of seventy school days a year from traveling. The school administration was fine with it, but Sierra's friends were not. They refused to include her in activities, including sitting together in the cafeteria. Sierra grew depressed. When Todd and I realized the extent of her sadness, we not only sought counseling as a family, but decided to pull both children out of public school. They never wanted to attend public school and for the seven years that they attended, Sierra and Bryce had asked every day to teach themselves.

Middle school years are very important and impressionable years and a decision made by a parent can hugely impact a child's life. I had to trust that I could maintain my livelihood as a writer and a bread-winner as well as keep my identity and not totally lose myself in the job of teaching my kids. Todd and I also had to believe that this was the best decision for our children, that we would not be harming them but "helping" them. Sierra and Bryce were not the only ones on a quest for self-knowledge; Todd and I also learned what kind of parents we wanted to be and how to be the best ones that we could.

The Schuylkill County Student Conservation Club proved to be a miracle healer. Sierra had found her tribe. She pushed herself way out there to become involved, be a team member and then a leader. As a result, she discovered her area of strength and her passion. As a parent, you don't always know. You go with your gut and your instinct. You listen to advisors. You listen to what your children are asking; you listen to their hearts. They will tell you what they need, sometimes in words and sometimes in actions.

From saving tadpoles to studying elk infected with brain worms, Sierra's big heart came to care for all living things. As she was led down rivers in canoes and across mountain ranges as a child, the land spoke to her and made her want to learn to live sustainably, to work to keep the planet clean and green. Every experience she had in the natural world built on it. She was blazing her own trail. Sierra's actions provided one of the best proofs that experiential education works. What appeared like recreation for our family all those years was essentially growing an environmentalist, a caretaker, and a spokesperson for life which had no voice.

When Sierra grew older and left home for a long period of time, she would pay a visit to both the Little Schuylkill River and Hawk Mountain's North Lookout. She said good-bye to the land but will revisit upon her return. It is her power source, like an electrical outlet that she plugs in to charge up. It was all those moonlight walks to North Lookout growing up, the river paddles, and the salamander hunts that cemented her to this land. These places, this source of nature, feed her psyche, and she uses them to derive strength. We all drain out as the world, its issues and its souls take from us. It is a wise person who comprehends this and does what is necessary to fill back up.

Sierra wrote the following essay before leaving home for Temple University in North Philadelphia. It illustrates not just her appreciation for her home and the natural world, but how it can influence who a person becomes.

My home is in the valley. I live at the foot of this mountain. Hawk Mountain rises up like a wall from my backyard. It is my sacred place. I have been coming here since I was a child. I can trace the trails that cover this mountain like the lines on the palm of my hand. I have favorite rocks, certain trees I always touch when I walk by. I scramble up the escarpment, the woods breaking on occasion to offer a view of the land at the foot of the mountain. The way I move up the path, hopping from boulder to boulder—one movement bleeding into the next is like a dance. I don't think about how I move. I memorized the choreography long ago.

My dance always ends at North Lookout. I stand on its shoulder, thrust forward on a precipice of rock. Hawk Mountain wraps its arms around a bowl of flaming orange trees. The hazy fields stitched together by carpets of forest are rolled out like a rumpled quilt.

I've been coming here long enough to notice the development,
houses like plastic Monopoly pieces lined up in clusters. Through this
valley and along the ridge runs the National Scenic Appalachian Trail,
a 2,150-mile long pathway stretching from Georgia to Maine, the
longest continuously marked footpath in the world. Both my parents
hiked this entire trail when they were close to my age, unaware of what
the future held—that one day they would live in its shadow and raise
two children who have come to love the natural world as much as they.

My bottom grows numb. I have been sitting on this boulder for
a long time. I feel as if I have become a part of the mountain. The
view, though startlingly beautiful to someone seeing it for the first time,
I sometimes take for granted and do not give it the appreciation it
deserves. I take in the view like I take in air. I am no longer conscious
of it. But just as I need oxygen filling my lungs, air to exist, the view
from Hawk Mountain also sustains me.

The more our family traveled internationally, especially to developing
countries, the more Sierra came to believe that you cannot separate the
care of the land and the animals from the indigenous people who have
lived there. At Temple University, she majored in Anthropology and
minored in Geography & Urban Studies, focusing on the environment,
particularly water issues. Sierra's leadership and her conservation club's
extensive work enabled her to earn two $10,000 private college scholar-
ships that sent her to Temple University.

Todd and I knew our children were very bright. They both had complained bitterly in elementary school that they were bored and so we had
them tested for the GAT (gifted and talented) Program. Although it is
very unusual, both kids scored high (in the upper 99 percent in the entire
country) in both math and writing. Almost always, one side of the brain
is dominant. Todd and I were puzzled where this braininess came from.

My friend Lee Reinert turned the light bulb on for us. Lee has her
PhD in psycho-educational processes and worked for years as a home-
school evaluator. Lee believed Sierra and Bryce's well-developed brains

were the result of where they spent their formative years—five whole summers of their childhood on the Continental Divide immersed in nature. Those trips presented them with an incredibly unique and radically influential classroom.

It wasn't many years into Bryce and Sierra's college careers until Todd and I both felt surpassed in intelligence. But we were way ahead of them when it came to wisdom; we had lived longer on the planet and had continued to learn and grow right alongside them. I remember when I came home for the weekend my freshman year of college. I felt proud of my new knowledge in sociology, psychology, and world religions and couldn't believe that my parents knew little in these areas. Todd and I never felt this pompous attitude coming from our own kids, however, just the utmost respect. Todd and I never professed that we had taught them *everything* that they needed to know in life before they fledged, but we did aim for the most important lessons, at least in our opinion.

There will be holes in any child's upbringing and education, things that slipped through the cracks. There is too much to learn in the world to think you can cover it in a mere eighteen years. It wasn't until Sierra was housesitting for a college professor and I came to visit that I learned how I had screwed up in the housekeeping part. My girlfriend recently bought me a plaque that read, "The way to avoid housework is to live outside." With this somewhat skewed philosophy as well as our funky lifestyle of living without many modern conveniences, complications were bound to occur. We were running out of time to educate them too!

At her professor's apartment, Sierra was opening the dishwasher to obtain clean dishes so we could enjoy our meal when she became baffled that the plates were not clean. "I ran the dishwasher," she said puzzled. "I'll have to do it again," and she closed the door and re-pushed the button.

"You need to put in dishwashing soap," I informed her.

"Really? How was I supposed to know that? How do *you* know that?"

"My mother had a dishwasher." I looked under the sink for the detergent, opened the trap door, and poured in the powder.

Sierra was impressed that I possessed this skill about technology that she did not. I tried not to laugh.

She told me earlier in the week that she had put her soiled clothing into a machine and turned it on and was surprised to find that the powdered soap just caked onto her clothing and the water never entered the machine. We don't have a clothes dryer at home. We have permanent clothes lines in our balcony library. The wood stove heat dries out the air and the wet wash puts much needed moisture into our house in the winter. Or, I hang my wash outdoors. Her professor's apartment-size washer and dryer looked alike, she rationalized.

Earlier in the week, her friend had to stop her from heating up food in an aluminum pie plate in the microwave. (We've never owned a microwave.)

"Mom, you failed!" she accused me.

"You can easily pick up these skills, bright child that you are, and bring yourself up to snuff," I assured her, laughing.

It's more important to teach your children to have confidence in themselves and to understand that learning how to learn is more important than the actual accumulated body of knowledge. For learning is an ongoing process and we will learn from others our whole lives. Every individual's body of knowledge that they leave home with reflects how they were brought up, what experiences they had and what their parents thought important to teach them.

A friend who was a National Outdoor Leadership School (NOLS) instructor told me he had a college student on an Alaskan kayak trip who was surprised to discover that Alaska was not an island like Hawaii, since it had its own square in the atlas like the Hawaiian Islands. It is doubtful that her family traveled much and probably spent zero time looking at maps or atlases, pondering the big world.

Another time, Todd and I were giving a voluntary simplicity workshop to honor students from Salisbury University in Maryland, and I had to stop a student who was stirring a large pot of refried beans by merely moving the top inch or two of the dense food. I told him he had to dig down to the very bottom and stir or the beans would stick and burn. I teased him and said, "Didn't you ever stir anything before?" "No," he answered.

I reiterated, "You mean you never stirred a pot of *anything* before?" and he repeated, "No." When dinner was over, another young man on dish washing duty ran the faucet at full speed and filled up every individual teaspoon with liquid detergent. That was his first time washing dishes, he said, and he had no clue. He probably was adept at working a dishwashing machine, however, unlike my child!

There are many different sets of skills. The life skills you need to function and be happy in one lifestyle can be much different when you are injected into another life situation. The unique skills Sierra and Bryce acquired in their childhood, like fording a river or staying safe from grizzly, taught them important lessons that bolstered their belief in themselves and their ability to learn. Of course, Todd and I had some doubts whether we taught them enough. Life will always be about learning new skills, including relationships that grow and flux with time. This fascination with the world and its people should never stop. Then you will be constantly awed by the world. If Sierra can travel to foreign countries on her own and learn to navigate unusual cultures, finding her way around a modern kitchen will be a cinch.

Actually, the biggest challenge in raising and educating Sierra was helping her overcome her tendency to be an over-achiever. Just possessing this self-knowledge enables you to be aware and work to balance your life. When in public school, she always strove for the 105 percent grade that came from extra credit. As a home-schooled student, she relaxed to a great degree but then picked up the pace again in college. If there was an award or scholarship or a grant to win, she won it, like the Udall Scholar, awarded to her twice for her leadership, public service, and commitment to the environment. When she missed the natural world in Philadelphia, she gave birth to the Temple University Outdoor Club and introduced hundreds of students to nature.

When Todd and I witnessed Sierra getting her golden honor cords placed around her neck at college graduation—where she also received the Diamond Award, the highest award the university bestows to a graduating senior—we felt very proud. How concerned we were when we decided to allow Sierra and Bryce to leave public school and teach themselves. I was afraid of falling short as a facilitator, afraid my children would get lazy and I'd have to fight them to do the work, afraid they wouldn't get into college. Nothing could have been further from the truth.

DECIDING ONE'S OWN PATH

As Sierra and Bryce learned about themselves over the years, Todd and I learned about *ourselves*, as parents, right alongside them. Learning who our son Bryce truly is, how to best raise and educate him as well as help him blaze his own trail was a different challenge for Todd and me. His creative mind often traveled elsewhere. He was often in another world, singing, rhyming, and daydreaming. As a result, he easily lost things. When Bryce was in public school, our family attended a hiking conference in New Hampshire and he realized he left his backpack three hundred miles away. He headed outdoors to wander in circles, sobbing, repeating, "Oh my God, I'm going to be in so much trouble. My teacher is going to be so mad at me."

I got on the phone and called the university, located it, and had it shipped home. When the book-bag arrived in the mail, I drove it to school and the secretary said, "What is waiting for him at home for all this?"

At first, I did not get it. "Cookies, hugs?" I thought. "Oh, along the lines of *punishment*?"

Punishment sounded absurd to me, especially as a mother who has led a life of forgetting, losing, misplacing, breaking things, and it only slowed a bit once I entered adulthood. I knew my child. I felt my son's pain. When seventeen-year-old Bryce was awarded a slot in a private art camp in Wyoming, he was forced to fly alone and he was very nervous. His fears were not completely ill-founded, for he accidently threw away his boarding pass at the airport McDonald's restaurant and had to frantically riffle through the trash receptacle to retrieve it before racing back to the gate.

When he attended college, he was nervous about negotiating the train home by himself but his father and I coached him through it. On one of his maiden voyages, he experienced a near-crisis. To pack for his weekend home, he used to toss all his belongings—school books, art supplies (loose X-ACTO knives, individual chalk pastels), dirty wash— into a large Mylar shopping bag. His wallet and cell phone also got tossed in (not a good choice).

He disembarked at the wrong station and realized it in mid-stride. His big bag, however, was still on the train, but he was off, and the long fabric handles were sandwiched in-between the closed train doors. What should he do? If he lets go, all his most important belongings will be lost. The train was about to pull out when the porter realized his dilemma and reopened the doors.

My son is brilliant but he is focused, and not necessarily on the reality at hand. I had similar challenges as a young person (although I was not nearly as bright and talented as Bryce). My mother did not get me. She misinterpreted my behavior and told me that I was stupid. Luckily, for my clear mind, I did not buy it. I knew I had a handicap but I was definitely not stupid. She admitted years later, that although she loved me very much, she did not know how to raise me.

I understood Bryce. And although I sometimes reacted as though I was exasperated, I was still laughing at the comedy of it all, and my heart went out to him. I empathized with his frustration of spending so much of his time looking for lost things.

I did not want to teach my child that he was stupid. I did not want to teach my child anything negative about himself. I wanted Bryce to possess the self-knowledge of who he is, understand why he behaves the way he does and love himself. We needed to look at this challenging characteristic and try to work with it, for no other reason than to make life a little easier for him and avoid a crisis in the future.

I would rather Bryce use his energy and brain to create beauty in the world. That was more important—to give the world something positive that it did not know it was missing. My accepting this trait of being scattered and his own acceptance of himself was a gift. His very thorough, tidy, and efficient father, on the other hand, would never criticize his wife or his son for their shortcomings. Although he does believe if we tried harder, we could live a more orderly life, be more productive with our time, and not spend so much of it searching for lost things. When your parent gets you, accepts you, supports you, and says, "It's alright. We can learn to work on this," this is teaching our children a very positive message about themselves. Bryce truly believes he is good and bright and certainly worthwhile (most definitely not stupid!) despite a handicap.

Contrary to his sister, Bryce could have more easily stayed in public school and managed if he had to. Boys don't behave as jealous and catty as girls. What he really missed during all those years enrolled in public school was the extra time to make art. He was fortunate to have six years of complete control over his studies, from seventh to twelfth grade. It was art and always art that fueled his life.

Before Bryce completed his senior year of high school, he was invited to attend the free three-week Bauen Art Camp in the Bighorn Mountains of Wyoming. Bauen Camp was designed to empower young artists, bringing kids from diverse backgrounds and ethnicities together for a common cause: to learn art. The camp wanted to include a representative from a coal mining area and although Todd and I were not miners we did live in Pennsylvania's anthracite coal country. The board still wanted to extend the opportunity to Bryce to attend.

The artistic campers hailed from New York City's Bronx, Chicago's south side, and the Navajo Nation, kids who were raised very differently than Bryce. Todd and I thought this was a fine opportunity for our son to stretch his wings and learn from other cultures right here in his own country. Todd and I felt confident about his going; Bryce was a bit concerned. Actually, he was even a little nervous about attending.

One of Bryce's favorite books as a youth was Louis Sachar's *Holes*, the story of Stanley Yelnats, who had been unjustly sent to a boys' detention center. The fictional Camp Green Lake had no water but it did have a lot of holes, which the bad boys had to dig all day, every day, to build character. Bryce read *Holes* seven times and saw the film made from the book nearly as many. He half-jokingly, half-seriously wondered if Bauen Camp was at all like Camp Green Lake. Although Bryce loved art, he had never been away from his family or his home for that long a time and was uncomfortable about not being able to communicate.

Bauen Camp proved to be an enlightening experience for Bryce. He gained valuable insight into the adult he was growing into and the unique gifts he has to offer to the world. He wrote the following piece for his English composition class at the local community college:

Most of the kids were from the city and appeared threatened by the lack of skyscrapers and pavement. Julio was a miniature thug, sporting bandanas, fake diamond earrings, and pimp hats. Manny and Nestor were from Boston and seemed equally stunned by their surroundings. Two of the kids had fathers who were in prison, and Malik had been selling drugs on the streets of Chicago at age nine. He had quite a few graphic stories involving knife fights and chases with policemen and dogs. Hearing their stories, I couldn't help but feel a world apart.

Many campers were fearful of nature. Insects such as grasshoppers were threatening and Manny would often circle the cabin, spraying absolutely everything with Febreze. How could I relate to their experiences? I lived in the woods, owned llamas and only used a knife at the dinner table. It wasn't long before I found out what I had in common—a love for hip hop culture. One afternoon a group of kids congregated in the barn to listen to rap music and take turns dancing. Entering the circle, I proceeded to break dance, which was followed by warm applause. It wasn't long before we were exchanging dance moves and holding freestyle rap competitions.

One day I was assigned to wash all the dishes for every meal as pun-ishment for skipping my cleaning duties. I was touched when Malik offered to help me out with the monumental task. Not only did it go faster with teamwork, but we invented some rap lyrics in the process: "You better wash those dishes. I'm not being fictitious. Don't act suspi-cious. The punishment is vicious."

"You help me, I help you," Malik explained. A day later I found myself repaying him for his efforts. On a day-hike into a nearby can-yon, we were divided into pairs. I ended up with Malik, who had never been on a real hike before, "except down to the corner store." We plodded along at a snail's pace on the well-maintained trail.

"Doesn't this scare you?" he questioned.

"Not really," I admitted. At least not as much as leaping fences while being pursued by cops.

Along our hike, we paralleled a stream, amid pines with vanilla-scented bark. Nestor and Manny were awestruck by it; to the same degree as me taking an afternoon stroll through the slums.

As the days past, people began to change. Manny's fear of nature transformed into a fascination. He went so far as to collect spiders and insects to observe their habits.

It was a sad day when the camp was over and we had to say our good-byes. Everyone was emotional. The inner-city kids were even crying.

Looking back, I can envision the bunk room at night as Nestor delivered his characteristic good-night.

"Manny, Goodnight my nigga. Kyle, Goodnight my nigga. Bryce, Goodnight my nigga."

"But I'm not Black," I pointed out.

"I don't care if you're not a nigga, you're still my nigga." Although we came from different backgrounds, from Chicago to the coal regions of Pennsylvania, from the hood to the wood, we all had something in common. We are artists and now we are friends.

Going to Bauen Camp had challenged Bryce, but he learned much more than art as he rubbed shoulders and bunked with these kids who were brought up far differently than him. He learned to find something in common, not focus on the differences which in this case, appeared blaringly obvious, but truly, not nearly as important in the long run, and he learned a little more about himself.

After his experience at Bauen Camp, Bryce learned of an opportunity to be an art camp counselor for Camp Dreamcatcher, in Bucks County, PA. This special summer program was for kids who are HIV positive or whose lives were impacted by the illness. Bryce was not only the art teacher, but helped the kids create a performance which included spoken word to express their positive experience at the camp. Although nearly every camper was Black or Hispanic, they saw no difference in this Caucasian boy who spoke their language and shared their spirit. This was one of the outcomes Todd and I hoped to accomplish as we led our children around the planet—to find similarities, not differences, amongst people. To build bridges, not walls.

As Sierra and Bryce approached adulthood, they became more self-knowledgeable and very clear on what kind of work they wanted to dedicate themselves to: Sierra in anthropology, geography, and writing; Bryce in art. Bryce still decided in his senior year to do a project shadowing fifteen different workers. Its purpose was not to explore potential occupations, but rather to educate himself on others' work and the role they play in society. We enlisted the help of our friends and used referrals and came up with an eclectic range of occupations. The list included: a machinist, dairy farmer, mortician, pharmacist, holistic vet, pizzeria owner, butcher, maintenance man, roof truss manufacturer, landscaper, vocational technical teacher, radio show host, truck driver, firefighter, and a bootleg coal miner. Bryce hoped that by spending the day immersed in these day-to-day jobs, he could gain a greater understanding and appreciation of our neighbors and what goes into making the world work. Here are two accounts:

Mortician

*We have to support people through the hardest part of their lives,"
Orwigsburg funeral director Wayne explains. "I will do anything I
can for them without breaking the law. If they want to bury a child
with a newly purchased tricycle, I'll make it happen. If a mother wants
to hold her stillborn child at its funeral, I'll do what I can." His eyes
nearly tear up as he goes into greater detail.*

*Before today, the word "mortician" brought to mind a hollow-
faced, morbid man clad in all black, certainly not this light-hearted
jovial fellow. Although there are no bodies to prepare today, Wayne
allows me to spend a couple hours learning the skills of a mortician.*

*Wayne permits me to hold a cardboard box labeled "William some-
thing," which rustles gently when I shake it. I set it down carefully; not
eager for Will to have a spill.*

*First, Wayne reveals the viewing room, rows of chairs facing the
area where the caskets rest, under pink lights that add a rosy tone to
the body. Next he shows me his make-up kit—a pink, plastic case that
had once been his wife's.*

*The morgue is spooky, a room packed with empty caskets. I study
a collection of urns, one or two which do look suspiciously like tissue
boxes. If you didn't feel like using the cemetery or the tissue box option,
a new method of transforming the remains into a "gem stone" through
a compression chamber is available. It might be eerie to wear human
remains as jewelry though. "That's a lovely stone you have there. What
kind is it?"*

"It's Bob."

*Wayne shows me the room where the embalming takes place. Bottles
of unidentified chemicals lurk on the backs of shelves, gleaming chrome
tools waits in drawers, and the operating table looks like a sacrificial
altar in the center of the room.*

*So, this is how it goes. Dead Bob gets shipped to the funeral home
and reclines on the operating table. He becomes a human pincushion
and is drained by metallic leeches, then gets pumped back up to his*

old self. Then Wayne breaks out the pink make-up kit and makes Bob look ready for Prom. Bob gets popped into the fridge for a couple days, maybe joined by one or two antisocial buddies. Then Bob makes his final appearance in a coffin, hopefully not looking like a drag queen with excessive make-up. Then he either gets boxed up with the crowd in the cemetery, burnt to fifteen pounds of ash, or possibly turned into bling-bling.

I ask Wayne if the constant exposure to death changed his views life and death.

"It makes you think about your own death all the time," he answers. "You realize that life is fleeting."

It takes a special kind of person to work in a funeral home—someone kind and compassionate enough to assist families through hardships, and with the stomach to endure the process of embalming. It is an important task, to present a final image of a loved one.

Firefighter

The Allentown Fire Department was Captain Joe Donmoyer's second home. Its occupants were his second family. The firefighter gang included a number of chubby men with heads round and hairless as hard-boiled eggs. They lolled on couches, cracking open soda cans and grazing on food constantly. The men were always teasing each other, belching and laughing like a room of Vikings. When the alarm sounds, these potbellied men move with the speed of gazelles. One moment they are devouring fruit salad, engrossed in a hockey game, the next they are charging billows of black smoke to rescue a toddler surrounded in flame.

In the middle of the night, I awoke to glaring lights as the firefighters dressed in supersonic speed. I went from comatose to frantic in a split second. Sirens wailed as we sped down the street, cars darting out of our path like fish before the maw of a shark. We screamed our way through red lights, careening around corners at high speed.

We spotted the billows of blackness from blocks away and witnessed flames dancing wildly. Two cars had collided head on and crumpled, one erupting in a burst of fire. Thankfully the occupants had been removed before the flames overtook them.

I don't understand how firefighters can catch any restful sleep on night shift. I became paranoid. I was jumpy as a deer. "You get used to it," Joe explained. "Rookies have problems, but for me, I can slip into a deep restful sleep in an instant. But the constant adrenalin rush is bad for you and makes you more susceptible to coronary disease." They admitted, however, that the adrenalin rush was the main attraction.

As Joe drove me home the next morning, he told me it was all worth it, he said, because nothing compares to the feeling of saving a child from a fire.

In Conclusion

My job-shadowing experience taught me valuable lessons about my own trail I hope to blaze in life but also deepened my respect for the billions of working folk. Working at the pharmacy taught me about patience when the days are repetitive. Witnessing the work of a holistic vet was evidence that there is always another approach to a situation. A day with the happy-go-lucky butcher taught me that it is all about attitude and with an optimistic outlook on life, any occupation can be tolerated. Witnessing the depression at the roof truss factory was proof that crushing economic times are taking a toll on everyone. Astonished by the grim conditions of the machine shop, I learned that to make society function, someone has to do the dirty work. When I drink a glass of milk, I imagine the hours spent slogging through cow manure before sunrise and the sacrifices that must be made. Until I spent a day with a landscaper, I never paid attention to the countless beautiful gardens and manicured lawns I passed in the car. Spending the day at the Vo-Tech center was proof that the future is shaped by the hands of teachers. A day with the mortician made me realize that some occupations require a special kind of person. Only someone who is kind-hearted and understanding could assist people through the pain of a losing a loved one. Driving into New York City in an eighteen-wheeler taught me that whatever you chose to do, be the best that you can be and that solitude can be a blessing. In contrast, a night with the Allentown Fire Company taught me that companionship can liven up an otherwise dull situation. Nightshift with the firefighters also taught me to always stay on my feet because life changes directions fast. Sometimes you have to hurdle through the red lights to get where you need to go. Sometimes you have to disregard the rules if it means saving a life.

Altogether, my job-shadowing experiences made me realize that my life of freedom comes at a price. It is paid for by the butchered hands of factory workers, the labor of sleep-deprived truck drivers, and the patience of teachers who inspire kids to seek these occupations."

Bryce got much out of his job shadowing experience because of his acute observation skills. Back when he and Sierra were on the Continental Divide Trail, both children learned to pay attention as they spent months and countless hours on the back of a llama. Both children also learned to pay attention by observing their mother as I practiced my craft as a travel writer and photographer. All the years we traveled as a family, I often worked on magazine articles at the same time. They saw how I took notes, listened as I interviewed people, watched as I composed photographs, and then afterwards, they edited my text. This was very important because it enabled them as young people to get out of their self-focused world and think about others. While I sought amazing learning experiences for my children, I not only showed them how to develop acute observation skills, they learned to cultivate a deep sense of curiosity about the world and its people. As we come to learn about others, we come to learn about ourselves too.

Bryce was able to better understand what it took to do the jobs of those he shadowed because of his clear self-knowledge. He was not afraid to take the risk and place himself in uncomfortable situations, in jobs which he had no prior experience; yet he was able to find common ground. He also realized, more so than ever, that he was responsible for selecting the occupation that spoke to his soul and did not just deliver a paycheck.

Getting accepted into a good university can be very challenging as there are many bright students competing for the same slots, all with excellent test scores and high grade point averages. Students have to do something out of the ordinary in order to shine above the rest and be noticed. We did not know it at the time, but when Sierra and Bryce signed up to teach themselves, it would become an advantage, rather than a liability, when it came time for college. It is difficult to measure the results of experiential learning. But since I required that they reflect and communicate through the written word about their learning, I had received valuable feedback. The way they learned and what they did with their education set them apart from the other applying students.

At first thought, it seemed strange that both our children chose a university that was located in an urban neighborhood like that of North Philadelphia. Temple's campus was relatively safe but just beyond the safe border, life was on the fringe. My children had to learn how to safely cross a street when they first went to Philadelphia. Obeying traffic signals was one of those life skills, like using a microwave, that they needed to pick up as adults. One of the reasons Sierra gravitated towards Temple, after visiting over a dozen liberal arts universities, was because on a single floor of the honors dorm, students from twenty different countries were represented. The diversity at Temple resonated with Sierra's heart. The dozen countries our family had traveled to before Sierra and Bryce set off for college created a need in them to be surrounded by different cultures, whenever possible. For Bryce, Temple's Tyler School of Art was all the reason he needed to attend. His beloved sister was also enrolled at Temple. And, Bryce loved the hip-hop culture that thrived at Temple and around Philadelphia.

As soon as we turned off Route 1 and onto North Broad Street in Philadelphia and saw the handful of young musicians playing drums in the middle of the street and collecting donations, Bryce knew he was "home" again.

Further down Broad, a church service revival was going on right on the sidewalk. There was lively singing and clapping as people spilled onto the street, smiling and singing the Lord's praises.

A few more blocks down, a couple sat on their front patch of grass at tables covered with yard-sale items and baked goods wrapped in plastic wrap. The husband-wife team sported look-alike red T-shirts and baseball hats and the husband had a Karaoke machine hooked up. He raised the mic to his mouth and tried to entice all us passersby to come up and buy a used coat or a Rice Krispy treat. "It's all right here folks. Stop by for a tasty treat while you check out these great barely used items."

Another few blocks down, a few women were creating an outdoor birthday party at a weedy vacant lot. Balloons were blown up and fastened to kitchen chairs carted from their homes, while coolers were brought in with refreshments. It was their local nature and they used what was available.

A smile moved across my face. My children have learned to flexibly move between their worlds, from Schuylkill County to North Philadelphia. I think it's important to not only function wherever you land, but also to bloom. As parents, we have to give our children the permission to strike out on their own path, allow them to develop into who they are destined to become, and while they are finding their voice, support and bolster them until they are strong enough to go it alone.

YOUR OWN PATH TO HAPPY

Ralph Waldo Emerson said, "To be yourself in a world that is constantly trying to make you something else is the greatest accomplishment."

Tyler School of Art is internationally recognized for its distinguished Graphic Design program. Although all the aspects of design, from type to web design, would assist Bryce in his future work, what he dearly loved to do was illustrate. He has not stopped drawing since he was four, when he picked up a tool and made his first drawing—a whale with a party hat. And contrary to the great majority of today's illustrators, Bryce still wanted to draw with a tactile tool in his hand—a pencil, an ink pen—old school. Not surprising when you look at how he was raised. There were no computer tablets up there in the Rocky Mountains, just a pad of paper and a pencil that his father had to sharpen with his pocket knife.

In Bryce's junior year of art school, his class's graphic design project was to create a make-believe restaurant with a theme, an accompanying menu, a take-out bag, and any extras the students could come up with. Bryce's called his restaurant "Beanstalk—Fairy Tales, Friends & Food," and he wrote all the copy related to fairy tales. Of course, it was creepy. Bryce wanted to make a fun pop-up menu and draw with a tool, as opposed to computer generated illustrations, and was alone in the entire school of graphic designers.

Throughout the course of the project, which lasted months, Bryce struggled with what *he* wanted to do, his vision, while also pleasing his professor. It was challenging to find a balance, for his professor was extremely hard to please. In critiques of Bryce's assembled menu, which was laborious to print and glue with the complicated pop-up additions, the professor would take a black marker and make large X's across the full menu, forcing Bryce to begin from scratch over and over again. It was disheartening for Bryce, to say the least.

When Todd and I attended the restaurant opening, we were thrilled to learn that Bryce won first place for his menu. When Todd and I met with Bryce's professor, his topic of conversation was Bryce's future as an illustrator.

"I know Bryce likes to illustrate and he is a very good illustrator, but it is an extremely competitive area to get into," said the professor.

And I said, "Well, that is what he has always wanted to do—write and illustrate books. For as long as he can remember."

"But is it so competitive. He really should take more computer classes. I've encouraged him to get into web designing first. That would be easier."

And I repeated, "Bryce does not want to design websites. He wants to illustrate with a tool in his hand. This is what makes him happy. And he certainly doesn't care about easy.'" About this time in the conversation, another mother walked by and said out loud to me, "Tiger Mother!" The woman was referring to the overpowering Chinese mother in the book, *Battle Hymn of the Tiger Mother,* by Amy Chua. That comment gave me a moment's pause. Was I a "Tiger Mother?" If what she meant was as a mother, I will fight tooth and claw for my child's right to choose his own path and will defend his decision, well then, I guess I am, but I don't think that's what she meant.

One more time the professor said, "It's just very, very competitive out there and I would not encourage him to start there."

Right about then, my blood pressure was rising and my mouth was about to say things that I may not have control over and might regret later. I was looking across the room at Bryce who was visibly sweating. I knew Bryce's professor did not have a clue as to how this budding illustrator had been raised—to seek happiness, value freedom and independence, and follow his heart. He also did not know that because of my son's talent and brains, he received enough scholarships that he did not have to worry about debt when he graduated and could be flexible in what he pursued. Todd and I never taught our children to seek after money. We didn't think money was important and that it would come to you if you did the work that you loved and you did it well.

When I was an art major at Indiana University of Pennsylvania, I had a painting professor who was very hard on me. After two years, I wanted to transfer to a professional art school, the Pennsylvania Academy of Fine Arts in Philadelphia, and I had only one painting class to show for myself. No matter how hard I tried and how diligently I worked, I received straight Ds for grades. I was very upset and confused. Why would they want me at the Academy with such a poor painting grade? I applied anyway, got accepted, and received a merit scholarship to attend. At the end of my last semester at Indiana, I received an A+ in painting. When I questioned my prof, he replied, "An A+ was the grade you truly deserved all along but I didn't think you would work up to your potential if I gave it to you."

Another student may have listened to the prof and the negative voices in her head. He could have set me on a downward spiral of thinking very little of myself. He could have smashed my dreams. Just like Bryce's professor could have directed him down a path that was not his true direction if he was not strong and did not believe in his own vision.

Bryce possessed enough self-knowledge to know what he wanted to do with his life, that which made him happy. Still, his confidence periodically lapsed and he asked, "Everyone in school is serving internships at graphic design firms. Do you think I should be too?" And I replied, "You don't *want* to be a graphic designer. You want to illustrate. Your life, your work, your job, can look *completely* different than everyone else's at Tyler. Never compare yourself to anyone. Never let anyone sway you to be someone else who does not resonate with your heart. You are on your own path to happy."

A graphic design artist/friend of mine for many years disagreed with me on how these types of professors treated their students. When Bryce first went to art school, he reported professors who were so hard on the students, who said how terrible they were, and habitually made students cry in class. They said it was done to sift the wheat from the chaff.

My artist friend said that this type of bullying was necessary. That this is the way it was going to be in the real world and as the parent, I should take the professor's side. I begged to differ. I did not believe any human being has the right to belittle another, especially a fragile student, especially a fragile freshman. It was so easy to fail at college. I believed we should be building one another up; there should only be supreme support, not trashing. That was how we chose to teach our children for twenty years and this was one of the most important things that we could pass on. Trashing does nothing positive for a person, especially a vulnerable young student who is trying very hard to believe in themselves.

Bryce, like his sister, graduated from Temple University with honors and received the Best Illustrator Award from Tyler School of Art. He went on to shape a successful career as an illustrator, right out of the gate.

SLIDE SHOW

The closeness our family experienced because of how Todd and I raised and educated our children became our greatest joy as parents. Our 3,100-mile-long llama pack trip is to thank for the initial idea that we could and should be our children's main educators. We didn't all just fall in love with lifelong learning, we fell in love with each other along the way. After Sierra and her future husband, Eben Yonnetti, hiked the Colorado Trail, she requested that I dig out my Continental Divide Trail multimedia show and share it with him. She wanted him to learn of this special part of her history, to better understand the events that went into creating who she is today. It had also been twenty years since we began our first leg of that five-summer-long adventure hiking the Colorado Trail.

When my book *Scraping Heaven*—about our family's long journey— came out in 2003, I had many speaking engagements. We even had a special gig in elementary schools, where we brought a llama right into the auditorium. We set up our tent, showed the students how we packed the llamas' panniers, and went through the gear that enabled our family to survive in the wilderness for months at a time. I talked about keeping a journal and how this became my actual job, writing about doing something that I loved.

We brought Sierra and Bryce along to every show. Our audiences wanted to see and meet them, ask them a question or two about how the experience impacted their lives. Our kids never got tired of reliving their wonderful memories up on the big screen. I had no idea how seeing the slide show years later would impact them or me.

My Continental Divide show is old school—two Kodak carousel projectors with a dissolve unit that fades images in and out with a turn of a knob. All eight songs in the show had their own unique timing and pacing. The four carousels might have slides missing, leaving behind empty slots which would project a shocking white screen. The old cassette tape might not pull, and did we even have a boom box in working order that accepted cassettes? Maybe the projector bulbs would be burned out or broken. I wasn't interested in practicing my timing. It was enough I was taking the time to dig out the equipment. Carrying all the equipment down the steps to the living room, moving furniture, setting up the projector screen, trying the music—it was also a lot of work. I had huge doubts that I could pull it off. I would *try*. That was all I was promising.

The stars were aligned. I found the correct carousels, and all the transparencies were there; I had two working projector bulbs, and the tape player worked. I first put the tape on to roll through and reacquaint myself with the music, but I was not prepared for what happened as soon as I heard the music.

I began to cry, and cry harder. The music unleashed a flood of memories, like someone opened up the sluice gates. When I put the show together many years ago, I chose moody music that would move my audiences emotionally. The accompanying images cycled through my mind: traversing Yellowstone, crossing Wyoming's expansive Great Divide Basin, the views from Glacier National Park, being together as a family, and on and on. I couldn't believe it. Over twenty years have passed since we began that grand adventure. I kept busy in the house, moving quickly, doing the dishes so no one would notice the tears streaming down my cheeks. Sierra was upstairs with Eben when the tape began to play, and she too was affected. Eben yelled down, "Sierra lit up as soon as the music came on." Lit up. Good word choice.

I had my slide show timing down perfect. Throughout the seamless presentation, both kids kept saying, "Oh my God, I remember that. That was so cool," and relayed wonderful stories as the slides faded by. The whole presentation spanned five summers of my children's early lives. Seeing their happy, smiling faces as they crossed high passes; Bryce dancing down the trail as Todd held his little hand; Sierra talking to her llama Berrick; images of storms we weathered, campsites we rested at, river fords we swam through—over three thousand miles of memories and five summers, year after year as the children grew up. Some of the most important moments of our lives together were being relived on that screen. The strongest feelings we were left with at the show's conclusion were feelings of happiness; actually, much more than happiness—outright joy of being together in the wilderness.

From Sierra's journal:

Watching the slideshow of our hike across the CDT/Colorado Trail was in many ways, a double return to my childhood. Memories of the trail, riding my llama, the rich smell of crisp mountain air, and the approach of thunderstorms were lifted from my memory. At the same time, I was brought back to the decade afterward that I followed those memories around to show after show that my mother gave. The repetition somehow made the memories richer, embedding them deeply inside of me. That part of me ached and came alive again as the pictures flashed across the screen. Although I was a child, somehow it felt like yesterday.

From Bryce's journal:

Watching the fluttering light of the projector, I entered a time warp. Each slide seemed to recover a submerged memory. It was a stirring experience. Sierra and I remembered the songs from when we joined Mom at presentations; they felt like the soundtrack to our childhood. Sierra and I laughed at the images of us dancing impishly on riverbanks, and marveled at the sweeping beauty captured in the predigital era. We noticed subtle changes we had never noticed before, like the grayness creeping into Dad's night-black beard. Now, twenty years whiter, Dad is no less of a mountain man.

I remember walking across the top of the world, windblown and surrounded by endless mountains, over rock as old as the earth itself, and I remember being terrified and humbled by the power of God and Colorado storms. I remember picking huckleberries after long rains in the cool solitude of the woods, feeling the spring of pine needles in light thick as honey, climbing through fog and turrets of stone that became trolls in the half-light, and watching aspen trees glimmer like fish scales beyond the meadows. I can still recall being entertained for hours by Dad's epic stories of "The Adventures of Sweetcakes" (Sierra's teddy). I remember specifically Sierra licking the entire rim of the Nalgene bottle, to ensure that I would either have to suffer to drink it or become dehydrated. I remember the smell of sagebrush, catching fish in meadow streams and singing songs all day. My music was the soundtrack of rain and marmot squeaks. I was alienated from the rest of society and for that I am grateful.

The Continental Divide literally traced the path of my childhood. My first experiences of the world were of the primitive connection to nature where I simultaneously realized my strength and significance. Two decades have passed since the trail and the years have been filled with fantastic trips and experiences. These have shaped who I am but remain incomparable to those first summers in the Rocky Mountains.

As I packed up my equipment, I felt dazed. The slide show took me back in time and then allowed me to fast forward through a large chunk of their lives. How could Sierra and Bryce's childhoods have gone by so quickly? The speed of the passing years was comparable to the flashing transparencies on the white screen. I dragged my feet to slow the circles of the years down. I had been cognizant of the great gift of their presence in our lives and of their desire to want to share their growing years with us, for not every parent is awarded that gift. But I couldn't stop time from passing by. Sierra was looking to get married soon and pursue a master's degree; Bryce was moving to Philadelphia to grow his illustration business and live with his girlfriend.

The finality of it slammed into me like a windstorm on the Divide. Our job was done. It really was over.

EPILOGUE

"Actually, the best gift you could have given her was a lifetime of adventures."
Lewis Carroll, *Alice in Wonderland*

As my sixth decade approached, the children were gone and I wanted to do something epic to usher in the second half of my life. Sierra was in Boulder, Colorado, in graduate school, with her new husband, Eben, studying geography on a National Science Foundation Fellowship. Bryce was in Philadelphia with his girlfriend, Calan, creating fabulous labels for micro-breweries. Todd and I were home alone, with not a lot of lively chatter, hip hop music, or buddies to drink coffee with. Instead, our home was too quiet, our life was too slow, and as we listened to NPR, we grew increasingly more depressed over the politics of our country. We were not embracing the empty-nest stage with open arms.

Todd was obsessed with chainsaw carving and creating beautiful creatures out of white pine chunks and he stayed mostly occupied with his art. I had this book to work on and had begun to do plein air painting again after many years, but it was not enough. I kept hearing Sierra's request when we went down to the Everglades that winter of 2011 to paddle the hundred-mile wilderness: "I want to do epic or it's not worth it."

So Todd and I decided, twenty-five years after we began the 3,100-mile Continental Divide Trail, that we would return to the Rockies. This time, however, we would mountain bike the range from Jasper National Park, Alberta to the Mexican border, on the Great Divide Mountain Bike Trail. The route is far different than the wilderness hiking trail. It mostly follows forest service gravel roads. We might cross the divide and sometimes multiple times a day, and we might do single track, rough and narrow where we have to push our loaded bikes, but it is a completely different experience. It would take us a few summers to complete the entire trek. One of the joys of this adventure is we would visit many of the passes and towns that we accessed as resupply points on the CDT. In fact, we contacted many of our old llama friends—those who were still alive—and are having one happy reunion after another as we ponder together, where *did* the time go?

In the summer of 2016, Todd and I bike-packed the first leg, eight hundred miles, down through the Canadian Rockies and northern Montana. Bryce joined us for the first week, kicking his parents off right. The summer of 2018, Bryce, Sierra and Eben rode the first two weeks with us and started their parents off right for another summer of adventure, clocking in another 500 miles. They are a joy to have along. We will return year after year until we reach the Mexican border.

In between summers of riding, Todd and I work at learning how to make fun without our kiddos, our best friends. It has been a tough haul, as challenging as mountain biking the Divide itself. We have to learn how to navigate alone again. We can't go back to who we once were, for the last twenty-five years of raising and educating kids has changed us. We have to find new joys, and reconnect with what we used to do before the children came along. I am working on upping the fun factor in my life because it felt like it took a nose dive after the kids left home. And so we are mountain biking 2,600 miles instead. Still, it is brand new territory ahead. We have to do it right and teach the kids that their parents have enough going for them as a couple that we won't succumb to depression and 1,000-piece puzzles.

It is wonderful that Sierra and Bryce care enough that they want to clear their schedules and still go on adventures with their parents and make more memories. That is the greatest compliment our children can give us. To choose to be in our company once they no longer have to. Todd and I did not teach them everything they needed to learn; we left some gaps and maybe even passed on a few mistakes, but we did get one part right and all the rest of their learning pales in comparison: Sierra and Bryce know that they are the sun and the moon and the stars to their father and me. Our love for them is unconditional and never-ending. You can't really go wrong in raising and educating your kids if you get that part right. Children are resilient. We saw that fording rivers and battling windstorms on the Divide. With any luck, they will return to grace our lives. After all, they have a few things to teach us!

REFLECTIONS FROM
SIERRA AND BRYCE

SIERRA, TWENTY-EIGHT

It was while riding on the back of a motorcycle in rural Nepal, on my way back from interviewing a farmer about the chronic flooding he and his neighbors had been suffering, that I had a realization. It had not been the two years of graduate coursework that I had just completed nor my prior degree in anthropology that had most prepared me for this research that I was doing for my master's thesis. I was living on an island in the middle of the Karnali River for two months while I tried to understand the history of this place's development and how social and economic politics were intertwining with climate change to produce chronic disasters. I had read many books over the years leading up to my research that had radically reshaped the way I understood the world. Classes in research methodology had helped me to design a strong thesis project. And yet, I realized that as a student of human geography, interested in the social dimensions of climate change and development, my methods—interviews, focus groups, and oral histories—essentially boiled down to talking with people and listening. I was on a basic search for understanding grounded in people's everyday stories.

I had learned the value of this kind of education—and the knowledge about the world that can be made by actively participating in it—not in any institution of higher education but as I grew up following my mother around as she interviewed people for articles, home and abroad. Watching her and joining her as she had these conversations taught me how to be curious, and how to engage in genuine conversation. My academic research today is how I continue to apply the iterative process of learning that I practiced as a child both at home and abroad. Actively participating in the world and communicating with others has always been my path to understanding.

I am currently in New Delhi, India as a Fulbright-Nehru student researcher on a grant funded by the US State Department and Government of India. I am working closely with the Jawaharlal Nehru University and the National Institute for Disaster Management as I research the traditional strategies communities have practiced over the centuries for coping with floods, droughts, and climate-induced crisis. While I am not immune to the anxieties of moving to a new place and living and working with different people—however exciting the adventure—I am convinced that the confidence I have today, even in the midst of much uncertainty, is because of the way in which I was raised and educated. The experiences that my parents gave me, not only all over the world but also in my own backyard, empowered me to put myself out there and made me a global citizen, comfortable living in and participating in multiple communities.

From this education, I came to know that it is just beyond the edge of our comfort zone where we grow the most. When we embrace uncertainty we also open ourselves up to experiences that often exceed even our wildest dreams. This is how I try to live my life and I find myself, now at the age of twenty-eight, still spending my days in pursuit of knowledge.

At the same time that my childhood, and the education my parents gave me, instilled the courage to extend myself and find community in distant places, it also taught me to invest in the places I call home. For me this has always been Pennsylvania's Appalachian Mountains and the rivers that flow from them. Beginning in high school doing conservation camps across my state and founding a student conservation club to do projects throughout my county, I learned that with education and exposure to issues that impact the world we live in also comes a responsibility for action. As members of a community—social or natural—we have a role and a say in how we continue to (re)make the world we live in. As a fifteen-year-old I learned about the history of anthracite coal extraction in the mountains I loved and how it had impacted the rivers I grew up swimming and playing in. I learned about development, habitat loss, and the expansion of impervious services—that were also impacting water quality. Clean water cannot be taken for granted.

When I went to college at Temple University in Philadelphia, more than 100 miles downriver from the headwaters of the Schuylkill I had grown up in, I had an idea, inspired by my education and my watershed. I wanted to teach other students, kids like me, who were going to school along the Schuylkill River about what was happening upstream, about what had happened to the river in history, and what was occurring today so that others would also be inspired to do something. I worked with an advisor in the history department to design an experiential college course that would take students on a trip throughout the watershed from the Schuylkill headwaters to its confluence with the Delaware River in Philadelphia.

When I got a job doing outreach and education for the Schuylkill Headwaters Association, a nonprofit organization based in Pottsville, Pennsylvania, I reworked the program for high schoolers and launched Schuylkill Acts and Impacts in 2013 with a team of ten students. The program is now in its fourth year.

In many ways, it was like coming full circle. The program itself embodies how I see my own education and think about the process more broadly. It is a cycle whereby we become informed about the world by participating in it, and with this knowledge are both empowered and gain the tools to change it. For me, it began in my own backyard learning about issues along the Schuylkill River and then building a community to transform it. The work I am doing today on climate change, flooding and disasters follows the same cyclical shape but just on a larger scale. I am now working with more expansive definitions of community (the planet and all humans) in order to address bigger and more eminent crises. It is to this global scale that I am drawn.

Fundamentally, what I learned from my childhood and the extraordinary education that my parents gave me, was how to actively care for my communities near and far. I see myself as part of something bigger as I learned about my place in the world and cultivated a sense of responsibility. This is how we both recognize privilege and face injustice.

And it is from this place of understanding, one that is constantly deepening through our new encounters with each other and the world around us, that we gain the chance to participate in and give back to our communities by working *with* each other to remake our world a better place than that which we were given.

BRYCE, TWENTY-SIX

When you think of a great adventure, do you ever think of a set time when it all happened? *Once Upon a Time* was written for a reason; the best told stories were meant to be limitless. As a child, time really isn't something you ever dwell on, and luckily, I never had to.

There was no formula or logical set of steps that my parents followed to raise us; our lives were built like the stories we read about, they were spontaneous. The unfamiliar was thrilling. I didn't anticipate the beautiful sights so much as the travel hiccups and storms, the "near death" incidents like scaling Half Dome in the rain.

Just the idea that we were throwing ourselves into an experience, and the understanding that it was beyond our control, was liberating, even at a young age. My parents gave Sierra and me everything, but most importantly they gave us the world.

That's not to say I didn't appreciate the comfort and structure that we returned to at home. If anything, travel made me look forward to it more. A hot shower never felt better than after a week canoeing with alligators. After days sleeping on wooden platforms, I could appreciate a bed with no monsters underneath. This varied lifestyle deepened my appreciation across the board, of home, of the open road, and of the work it takes to create a life where you can balance both.

I'm working on this now, as I manage a freelance illustration business, balancing clients and deadlines. Currently I'm designing labels for breweries and distilleries, but I've illustrated everything from restaurant logos to snowboards. Much of this work borders on the creepy and surreal. When every brewery is competing to grab your attention, this presents a good outlet for an artist to pour out bizarre imagery.

My art is often influenced by past travels, the memories showing up unexpectedly in the detailed lines. I'll recognize the face of an old man in a Sicilian market, or the stone spires of Cappadocia, sneaking their way into the background of a label design. Travel journals are filled with portraits, stacks of resource to literally draw from.

The art of other cultures also inspired new styles of illustration. In Thailand, I remember being amazed by the gold leaf-covered temples. I would incorporate details into my work, the roof structure of a building or an eyebrow arch in a mask. What defined people and places constantly changed, and this was reflected in the details. Stick-figure drawings became something more after growing up surrounded by different styles of clothing; houses changed shape after seeing stilt-legged homes in Vietnam.

While travel influenced the artist I am today, Sierra's interests were sparked in other areas, namely anthropology and geography. This would be the case for every individual, regardless of their personal interest. I remember my dad's face lighting up when he walked through the woodworking section of town markets. While my parents were craning their necks up at the architecture in Prague, I was people-watching on the street, marveling "Did you see that guy's nose?" Whether your passions are carpentry or caricatures, travel fuels inspiration across the board.

A plane ticket overseas isn't a requirement—simply venturing outside your door can be a strong influence. I was equally inspired by the characters at our local farmer's market and passing strangers on the trails behind our home. Steps away from the bustle, I found solace in the natural world; endless variety of plants, rocks, insects, and weather was an artist palette to pick and choose from.

These experiences propelled me towards becoming an illustrator and pushed me to build a diverse portfolio with every new adventure. I was ready to blaze my own path, but little did I know that would lead me to Tyler School of Art. Replacing a log cabin in the woods with a shared dorm room in the center of North Philly wasn't the easiest of transitions.

There were so many new challenges presenting themselves, luckily I had the foundation of growing up on the Continental Divide Trail. No hordes of buffalo on Temple University's campus, just mobs of dazed students trying to find their classes.

While in one of my five-hour drawing classes, I daydreamed back to one of my favorite drawing memories. I remember finding a cow carcass along the CDT. Overjoyed, I drew faces on the bones and paraded them around in a puppet show. My parents weren't too amused, but they knew a future "demented" artist when they saw one.

Despite the long days and inconsistent sleeping schedule, quitting wasn't a realistic option. Many times on the trail there was no choice but to move forward, whether we were outrunning a thunderstorm or fording a river. That same forward motion is what helped fuel me through all-nighters in Tyler's graphic design lab.

Philadelphia has remained my home. I love the energy of the city, and Fairmount Park is only a bike ride away, offering the occasional nature fix. In a profession that demands that you be attached to screens, getting outside is a necessity. My eyes can rest on a nearby tree limb and I'll remember back to my imagination as a kid. That branch would become a rifle or a conductor's baton, an abandoned horseshoe would transform into Captain Hook's missing hand; anything was possible.

Although the natural world shows me that there is no ceiling for imagination, it keeps me grounded as well. When you're on a mountain ridge trying to outrun a lightning storm, the world becomes a lot bigger than you. You realize what you can control and what you can't. Extreme adventure isn't the only way to be reminded of this; looking up at the stars, or standing in your front yard in a summer storm is a quick way to come to terms with the scale of life.

Nature leaves you humbled, at your vulnerability and the passing time; it's hard to believe that twenty years have gone by since we finished the trail. Every so often people ask me "Do you remember anything from it?" I reflexively answer yes, but in my mind the word *memory* is loosely defined. I'd like to think I remember seeing the world from my dad's backpack. But for the most part I don't recall distinct moments so much as sensory impressions, like the thrill of walking a ridge-line, or the immense silence of waking up in a river valley.

It's not so important whether I can retain a specific memory. What matters are the lasting values this way of life has instilled in me, and the appreciation for charting an uncommon path. Wherever the road leads, I hope to walk it with an adventurous spirit. Nature will remain a library of resource for me. My parents used the world as our classroom, and it's a school I never plan to graduate from.

ACKNOWLEDGEMENTS

I would first like to thank my family, my husband Todd and my two children, Sierra and Bryce, for allowing me to share your stories with the world, especially when you are much more private than I am. It is a privilege that I do not take for granted and I am hugely appreciative. The memories that we created as a family, over and above what this lifestyle taught us, are the greatest gift. You are my best friends and my favorite traveling companions on the planet. I'd go anywhere with you and try anything.

I would like to thank the administrators and teachers at the Blue Mountain School District who granted me their blessing to take my children out of school to travel and learn from the big world. I know you made many exceptions, and I appreciate the deep level of trust you put in us as we went against school policy. You believed first in the best education possible for my children. You gave us the best of both worlds in the years where Sierra and Bryce juggled both public school and world school at the same time.

Thank you to my readers/editors who are my personal friends—Lynne Williams, Lee Reinert, Maryalice Yacutchik, Kim Harnish, and my two children, Sierra and Bryce—who read every word of every chapter as well as every version of the book, and there were many! There were many more friends who helped with individual chapters, as I asked their advice and input, too many to mention here but you know who you are. Thank you for your time and expertise.

A big individual thank you to my girls, Lee Reinert and Lynne Williams, who served as home school evaluators, personal advisors, and overall cheerleaders, encouraging me to raise and educate our children in this alternative way. You gave us the confidence to believe we could be the best teachers for our kids and supplied the tools on how to do it.

I would like to thank my literary agent, Charlotte Cecil Raymond, who worked with me on my fifth book, *Kids in the Wild: A Family Guide to Outdoor Adventure*. She got back in touch at the beginning of this long book endeavor and asked what new projects I was working on. She told me that she believed in my message and wanted to continue to work together and support my efforts. I am very glad we joined forces to make *The World Is Our Classroom* a reality.

Thank you to the editors at Skyhorse—Olga Greco and Jon Arlan, who worked their magic and made *The World Is Our Classroom* even better. I appreciate your wisdom, skill, and friendship.